eat

For my family and friends – and the many wonderful dinners we've shared

First published in 2003 by New Holland Publishers (NZ) Ltd
Auckland • Sydney • London • Cape Town

218 Lake Road, Northcote, Auckland, New Zealand
14 Aquatic Drive, Frenchs Forest, NSW 2086, Australia
86–88 Edgware Road, London W2 2EA, United Kingdom
80 McKenzie Street, Cape Town 8001, South Africa

www.newhollandpublishers.com

Copyright © 2003 in recipes: Ray McVinnie
Copyright © 2003 in photography: Kieran Scott
Copyright © 2003 New Holland Publishers (NZ) Ltd

ISBN: 1 86966 022 6

Publishing manager: Renée Lang
Design: Gina Hochstein
Editor: Barbara Nielsen

McVinnie, Ray.
Eat / Ray McVinnie; photographed by Kieran Scott.
Includes index.
ISBN 1-86966-022-6
1. Cookery. 2. Food habits. I. Scott, Kieran (Kieran Edward). II. Title.
641.8—dc 21

10 9 8 7 6 5 4 3 2 1

Colour reproduction by Colourscan (Singapore)
Printed by Craft Print Pte Ltd Singapore

eat

Ray McVinnie

photographed by Kieran Scott

NEW
HOLLAND

contents

introduction

Eat is a personal collection of the kind of food I like to cook and serve to my family and friends, divided here into three categories. Starting with small plates, these dishes are for times when you want the first of a series of courses for a meal – or when you are planning a lighter meal such as lunch. Large plates (often comprising two or three easy recipes combined to make a more substantial dish) are for when you want a main course or a one-course meal. The last category, sweet plates, offers treats to finish off a meal, or perhaps mark a special occasion. Keen cooks can decide for themselves how to mix and match, and on what kinds of occasion they might serve their choice of dish or dishes.

To reinforce the idea that a recipe should not be seen as a rigid formula, and that cooking is much more than just a matter of following instructions, I have included plenty of suggestions for variations and accompaniments. Home cooks can use these as they please – but their main purpose is to provide ideas for following one's own inclinations regarding food, an essential quality in any good cook.

Being a good cook doesn't necessarily mean using complicated recipes or difficult techniques. It is often simply a matter of using the highest quality ingredients you can afford and preparing them carefully and simply. If I have little or no time to cook, I serve something simple but make sure it is the best quality I can find at the time. Save more adventurous cooking for when you can do it well, using ingredients you respect. The best ingredients are usually those you know you can trust because you know where they came from and how they were made or grown; for example foodstuffs certified as organically grown or produced are generally a good indication of quality.

In my experience shared dining is central to human wellbeing. There is nothing like sitting around a dining table sharing good food with family and friends. It is a relaxing time to exchange ideas, to learn to listen and be enriched by other people's stories, and for young people to learn those crucial social lubricators, otherwise known as manners. Even the most routine shared meal times are important. Their very continuity is reassuring, giving a fulfilling structure to busy lives, and they offer the perfect way to celebrate important occasions.

The recipes in this book are the result of some wonderful travel experiences and, of course, many delicious shared meals. For me they illustrate the exciting choices open to everyone who gains enjoyment and satisfaction from cooking and eating.

Ray McVinnie

small plates

Served solo, any one of these recipes could be an appetite-teasing first course or just the right size for a light meal such as lunch, while a combination could turn a meal into a sequence of tasty small courses.

Caren's Yoghurt Soup

This traditional Iranian cold yoghurt soup comes from food and wine writer Caren Davidkhanian, an Iranian-Armenian friend who lives in Rome. The sweet and sour flavour is complex, unusual and quite addictive. It's the perfect food on a hot day, but even in cold weather this dish is a restorative and an appetite teaser.

Serves 6

1 litre (35fl oz) plain unsweetened yoghurt

3 cloves garlic, finely chopped

1 cucumber, peeled, seeded and grated

75g (3oz) walnut pieces, crushed slightly
    under the blade of a knife turned
    on its side

75g (3oz) raisins

3 tablespoons chopped dill, plus extra for
    garnishing

6 large ice cubes

flaky sea salt and freshly ground black
    pepper to taste

for garnish

1 spring onion, green part only, finely sliced

Mix all the ingredients together except the spring onion, seasoning well with salt and pepper, and put in the refrigerator for about 2 hours to let the flavours develop.

Remove from the refrigerator and mix well. The ice will have melted enough to dilute the soup to a creamy consistency but will still be in lumps.

Serve in bowls with some sliced spring onion and chopped dill sprinkled on top.

or *leave out the ice and use the soup as a dip for warm flatbread*

or *use it as a side dish for a fish curry*

or *use it as a sauce for barbecued lamb.*

Ajo Blanco de Malaga

This chilled sweet and sour soup is the perfect thing to stimulate a jaded appetite on a hot day and is a simple purée of the common produce of Andalucia – almonds, olive oil, bread, vinegar and garlic. I can remember seeing recipes for it before I tasted it in Spain and thinking that such a dish could never work. How wrong I was! *Serves 6*

2 cloves garlic
225g (8oz) finely ground blanched almonds
150g (5oz) fresh white breadcrumbs
100ml (3 ½ fl oz) non-peppery extra virgin olive oil
about 3 tablespoons sherry vinegar
1 litre (35fl oz) iced water
flaky sea salt to taste
300g (10 ½ oz) seedless white grapes, halved

Put the garlic, almonds, breadcrumbs, and olive oil into a food processor and purée to a smooth paste. Add the vinegar and water and process until frothy. Taste and season with the salt. Pay attention to the sweet and sour flavour and add more vinegar if necessary.

Serve each portion of soup with a small handful of grapes in the bowl.

or *serve peeled, seeded melon (watermelon, green Prince melon and rock melon are all suitable) in the soup instead of grapes*
or *add half a peeled, seeded cucumber and a handful of mint leaves to the soup when puréeing*
or *omit the grapes and serve some thinly sliced poached chicken breast in the soup.*

Indian-spiced Vegetable Soup

There is nothing so restorative as soup – it is the ultimate comfort food. This is a delicious first course of slow-fried vegetables and aromatic Indian spices puréed with tomatoes.

Freshly ground spices have a much better flavour than ready-ground spices, and toasting them adds another dimension of flavour. *Serves 6*

2 tablespoons coriander seeds
2 tablespoons cumin seeds
¹/₄ teaspoon fenugreek seeds
1 teaspoon fennel seeds
3 tablespoons peanut oil
3 tablespoons finely chopped ginger
6 cloves garlic, finely chopped
finely grated zest of 1 lemon
1 teaspoon ground turmeric
1 cinnamon stick
2 small dried red chillies, finely chopped
2 onions, chopped
1 carrot, chopped
250g (8 ³/₄ oz) peeled, seeded, chopped pumpkin
2 medium-sized floury potatoes, peeled and chopped
400g (14fl oz) Italian canned tomatoes, mashed
1 tablespoon sugar
1 teaspoon flaky sea salt
1 litre (35fl oz) water
coconut cream or sesame oil for serving
chopped coriander
pappadums

Toast the coriander, cumin, fenugreek and fennel seeds separately in a dry frying pan until fragrant and slightly darkened in colour, and pound in a mortar or grind to a fine powder.

Heat the peanut oil in a saucepan over a moderate heat and add the ground spices, ginger, garlic, lemon zest, turmeric, cinnamon, chillies, onions, carrot, pumpkin and potatoes. Sauté without browning until the onions are soft. Add the tomatoes, sugar, salt and water, bring to the boil and simmer until the vegetables are tender.

Remove from the heat, discard the cinnamon stick, purée until smooth in a food processor, taste and check the seasoning. Put back into a clean saucepan and bring to the boil so that it is hot.

Cook the pappadums by simply putting them on a rack in a hot oven (200°C /400°F) until puffed, crisp and slightly browned – they take less than a minute to cook.

Serve the soup drizzled with either a little coconut cream or sesame oil, a sprinkle of chopped coriander and the pappadums on the side.

or *panfry a couple of diced chicken breasts in a little peanut oil and add to the soup*

or *poach any combination of seafood in the soup after it is puréed*

or *double the amount of vegetables, check the seasoning and turn it into a vegetable curry served with rice as part of an Indian meal.*

Thai Chicken and Coconut Soup

A version of Tom Kha Gai, the traditional Thai soup, given to me a few years ago by the chef at the Banyan Tree resort on Indonesia's Bintan Island. I have never met anyone who did not like this soup.

Galangal, kaffir lime leaves, lemongrass and canned straw mushrooms are available from Asian food shops. Fresh ginger doesn't have the same flavour as galangal but it will do as a substitute. *Serves 6*

*650ml (23fl oz) well-flavoured liquid
  chicken stock*
*3cm (1 1/4 in) piece fresh or frozen
  galangal, thinly sliced*
4 kaffir lime leaves
1 thick bulb lemongrass, squashed slightly
*3 tablespoons finely chopped
  coriander root*
3 small dried red chillies, chopped
5 very thinly sliced shallots
*1 double skinless, boneless chicken
  breast, thinly sliced across the grain*
*425g (15oz) can straw mushrooms,
  drained and rinsed in cold water*
400ml (14fl oz) coconut milk
100ml (3 1/2 fl oz) fresh lime juice
3 tablespoons fish sauce
coriander leaves for garnish

Put the stock, galangal, lime leaves, lemongrass, coriander root, chillies, shallots and chicken into a saucepan and bring to the boil. Simmer for 10 minutes, then discard the lemongrass.

Add the mushrooms and coconut milk and simmer for 3 minutes. Add the lime juice and fish sauce and mix well.

Serve in small warm bowls and sprinkle with coriander leaves.

*or put a large handful of hot, thin, cooked
  noodles in each bowl and serve the soup on
  top like a sauce for a more substantial dish*
*or double the amount of chicken and serve it on
  a bed of rice*
*or replace the chicken with prawns or a mixture
  of seafood such as diced fish, scallops,
  mussels, oysters or crayfish.*

Sopa Verde a la Morunna

Ever since I spent time in Spain I have been fascinated by the Arab or Moorish influence on southern European cooking. The combination of delicious, familiar Mediterranean flavours and spicy North African tastes is a successful fusion quite unlike any other.

This is an aromatic green spicy soup. It is served with a dollop of salty hot green olive paste. *Serves 6*

Olive Paste
20 pitted green olives
1 clove garlic
1 handful coriander leaves
1 small fresh green chilli
flaky sea salt

Pound together or put in a food processor the olives, garlic, coriander leaves and chilli and process to a smooth paste. Taste and season with salt. Set aside.

Soup
5cm (2in) piece ginger, peeled and
*   chopped*
6 cloves garlic
4 tablespoons chopped coriander root
*   and stalks*
3 tablespoons toasted cumin seeds
1/2 teaspoon ground cinnamon
4 tablespoons extra virgin olive oil
2 onions, finely chopped
4 courgettes (zucchini), cut into
*   1cm (1/2 in) dice*
4 large vine-ripened tomatoes, cored, tops
*   nicked in a cross shape*
1 litre (35fl oz) well-flavoured liquid
*   chicken stock*
2 handfuls spinach leaves, chopped
1 handful rocket leaves
3 tablespoons chopped parsley
flaky sea salt and freshly ground black
*   pepper*

Pound together or put in a food processor the ginger, garlic, coriander root and stalks, cumin seeds and cinnamon and process to a smooth paste.

In a saucepan heat the olive oil over a moderate heat and add the paste, onions and courgettes. Cook gently until the onions are soft.

Drop the tomatoes into boiling water for 20 seconds, then drain them, cool with plenty of cold running water, slip the skins off and chop into pieces. Add the chopped tomatoes and chicken stock to the pan and bring to the boil.

Add the spinach, rocket and parsley and simmer for 4 minutes. Taste and season with salt and black pepper.

Serve the soup in warm bowls with a spoonful of the olive paste in each.

or *add 400g (14oz) skinless, boneless firm white fish fillets with the green vegetables and simmer until the fish is just cooked*

or *use the olive paste as a rub all over chicken breasts or a whole chicken before roasting in a hot oven*

or *turn the soup into a substantial main course: make little meatballs out of 500g (1lb 2oz) finely minced lamb, a little garlic and mint, brown them in a little oil and finish cooking them in the soup when you add the tomatoes and stock, then serve the meatballs in the soup over rice.*

Tomato, Chickpea and Bean Soup

This is a storecupboard soup made with a flavour-base of gently fried vegetables and herbs bulked out with canned tomatoes and beans. Hearty soups like this one should be as thick as a stew – like the ones I first came across in restaurants in Florence. *Serves 6*

3 tablespoons extra virgin olive oil
2 tablespoons finely chopped tender tips of
   rosemary sprigs
4 cloves garlic, finely chopped
1 onion, finely chopped
1 carrot, finely diced
1 stick celery, finely diced
2 x 425g (15oz) cans red kidney beans
300g (10 1/2 oz) can chickpeas
2 x 400g (14oz) cans Italian tomatoes in
   juice, mashed
750ml (30fl oz) well-flavoured liquid
   chicken stock
flaky sea salt and freshly ground
   black pepper
chopped flat-leafed parsley

Heat the olive oil over a moderate heat and add the rosemary, garlic, onion, carrot and celery. Fry gently until the onion is soft.

Add the beans, chickpeas, tomatoes and stock. Bring to the boil and simmer until the carrot is cooked. Taste and season with salt and pepper.

Serve sprinkled with parsley.

or serve with short tubular pasta and a sprinkling of freshly grated parmesan cheese for a hearty main course

or chop a large handful of spinach leaves and stir them through the soup with the tomatoes as a variation, and serve with a dollop of plain yoghurt instead of parmesan cheese

or steam open 20 small live mussels, scrubbed, beards pulled out, in a little white wine, reserve the cooking liquid, shell and thinly slice the mussels and stir into the soup with some of the liquid to taste.

Zuppa di Riso

I was particularly taken with the hearty soups in the north of Italy. This one is like a soupy risotto. If you can't get pancetta, bacon will do. *Serves 6*

4 silverbeet (Swiss chard) leaves
4 tablespoons extra virgin olive oil
1 onion, finely chopped
1 small carrot, finely diced
1 stick celery, finely diced
3 cloves garlic, finely chopped
100g (3 1/2 oz) finely diced pancetta
finely grated zest of 1 lemon
200g (7oz) Italian rice (I like the vialone
    nano variety)
4 tablespoons dry white wine
1.5 litres (2 pts 10 1/2 fl oz) well-flavoured
    liquid chicken stock
1 handful spinach leaves, thinly sliced
flaky sea salt and freshly ground
    black pepper
freshly grated good quality parmesan
    cheese for sprinkling

Remove and discard the thick stems from the silverbeet, chop the leaves, boil in plenty of salted water until tender, refresh under cold water, squeeze dry and chop again.

Heat the olive oil over a moderate heat and add the onion, carrot, celery, garlic, pancetta and lemon zest. Fry gently, without browning, until the onion is soft.

Add the rice, mix well, and cook gently for 4 minutes. Add the wine bring to the boil and boil until the wine has evaporated. Add the stock, bring to the boil, and simmer for 25 minutes until the rice is well cooked.

Add the spinach and silverbeet and simmer until the spinach is tender. Taste and season with salt and pepper.

Serve with plenty of parmesan cheese sprinkled on each portion.

If you leave the soup to stand, the rice will continue to absorb the liquid and the soup will become very thick. If this happens, you can eat it like a wet risotto or add a little water to thin it, bring it back to the boil, taste and check the seasoning.

or *double the amount of pancetta and add a 400g (14oz) can of well-rinsed and drained borlotti beans when you add the spinach and silverbeet – this will turn the soup into a substantial one-pot meal*
or *add 2 handfuls of shelled prawns for a luxurious touch*
or *turn the dish into a risotto by cutting back the stock to 750ml (27fl oz) and bringing it to the boil before adding it one ladleful at a time, stirring until the liquid is completely absorbed before adding the next ladleful.*

Eolo Seafood Soup

I ate an excellent soup like this of slow-cooked vegetables with stock, seafood and greens in the Eolo restaurant in Amalfi. *Serves 6*

6 silverbeet (Swiss chard) leaves

3 tablespoons extra virgin olive oil, plus extra for drizzling

3 cloves garlic, finely chopped

1 small bulb fennel, cored and thinly sliced

1 small leek, thinly sliced

finely grated zest of 1 lemon

125ml (4 1/2 fl oz) dry white wine

1 handful spinach leaves

1 litre (35fl oz) well-flavoured liquid chicken stock

12 small live mussels, scrubbed, beards pulled out

300g (10 1/2 oz) skinless, boneless firm white fish fillets, such as monkfish, snapper or hapuku, thinly sliced

8 scallops, sliced almost in half

6 slices toasted ciabatta or other white sourdough bread

Remove and discard the thick stems from the silverbeet, chop the leaves, boil in plenty of salted water until tender, refresh under cold water, squeeze dry and chop again.

Heat the 3 tablespoons of olive oil over a moderate heat in a wide, deep saucepan. Add the garlic, fennel, leek and lemon zest and fry gently, without browning, until the leek is soft.

Add the wine and bring to the boil. Add the silverbeet, spinach, stock and mussels and bring to the boil. Simmer until the mussels start to open. Add the fish and scallops and continue cooking until the mussels are open and the fish and scallops are cooked.

Put a slice of toast into each of six hot wide soup plates and serve the soup on top. Drizzle with extra virgin olive oil.

or *serve the soup with a spoonful of chopped, cored, seeded tomatoes on top*

or *instead of a mix of seafood, use 600g (1lb 5oz) white fish only, or use just mussels or just scallops or prawns and oysters*

or *serve the soup over steamed rice and turn it into a meal.*

Spicy Mussels with Coconut Broth

Mussels are cheap and readily available, and their rich flavour makes a good first course. Here they are steamed open on a South-East Asian-style curry paste, which is slowly cooked first by gently frying in a wok. *Serves 6*

4 small dried red chillies
1 cinnamon stick, broken up into
    small pieces
125ml (4fl oz) boiling water
4 tablespoons peanut oil
3 tablespoons tamarind concentrate
1 teaspoon shrimp paste
5cm (2in) piece peeled ginger, chopped
10 cloves garlic
1 tablespoon ground turmeric
3 teaspoons finely grated palm sugar
4 sticks lemongrass, bulbous ends only,
    peeled and crushed
3 kaffir lime leaves, central spine removed
36 live mussels, scrubbed, beards
    pulled out
400ml (14fl oz) canned coconut cream
flaky sea salt

Soak the chillies and cinnamon in the boiling water for 20 minutes.

Put all the ingredients except the mussels, coconut cream and salt into a food processor and purée to a smooth paste.

Heat a wok over a moderate heat and add the paste. Gently fry the paste, stirring frequently, for 10 minutes until fragrant, reduced in bulk and starting to look greasy.

Add the mussels, mix well and turn the heat up. Cook until all the mussels have opened, removing them to a warm platter as they do so.

Add the coconut cream to the wok. Mix well. Gently bring to the boil, then turn down to a simmer and simmer for 2 minutes. Taste and season with salt if necessary, but remember the mussel liquid will be salty.

Put six mussels and some sauce into each of six small bowls and serve.

or *use the curry paste on which this dish is based for a chicken or fish curry.*

For chicken curry, brown chicken pieces in hot peanut oil, remove, make the paste and fry it, then add the chicken and a little water. Bring to the boil and simmer for 15–20 minutes until the chicken is well cooked and most of the water evaporated. Finish by adding the coconut cream, and serve with rice.

For fish curry, fry the paste as in the recipe then add 500g (1lb 2oz) skinless, boneless firm white fish fillets cut into 5cm (2in) pieces. Add the coconut cream, bring to the boil, simmer until the fish is cooked, and serve with rice.

or *use the curry paste to bake a whole fish. Mix the paste with enough coconut cream to make a pourable sauce and pour it inside and all over a medium-sized whole scaled, gutted fish, such as a snapper or gurnard, in a large roasting dish. Cover with tin foil and bake at 200°C (400°F) for 15–20 minutes or until the fish is just cooked, then serve with rice and a crunchy salad.*

Pappa al Pomodoro with Barbecued Mussels in Prosciutto

Two simple recipes served together in a wide soup plate make this a delectable first course or lunch. The mussels can be prepared in advance and cooked when needed. The Pappa al Pomodoro is a thick traditional Italian soup ('Pappa' just means 'mush' or 'baby food') and is an easy combination of briefly cooked tomatoes and basil. Because this is such a simple dish, use the best quality ingredients you can find.
Serves 6

Mussels
24 live mussels, scrubbed, beards
*   pulled out*
125ml (4fl oz) white wine
2 cloves garlic, crushed
24 paper-thin slices prosciutto
olive oil

Put the mussels, wine and garlic into a saucepan and bring to the boil. Boil until the mussels open and remove them as they do.

Discard the liquid. Shell the mussels and pull out the dark brown tongue. Roll each mussel up in a slice of prosciutto and secure with a tooth pick.

Heat a barbecue until hot and brush the mussels with olive oil. Barbecue until hot and browned. Serve on the following soup.

Pappa al Pomodoro
10 vine-ripened tomatoes, cored, tops
*   nicked in a cross shape*
4 tablespoons extra virgin olive oil
4 cloves garlic, finely chopped
large pinch of ground dried red chillies
1 tablespoon tomato paste
2 handfuls bite-sized pieces torn up
*   ciabatta or other white sourdough bread*
1 small handful basil leaves, torn into
*   small pieces*
flaky sea salt and freshly ground
*   black pepper*

Drop the tomatoes into boiling water for 20 seconds, drain them, cool with plenty of cold running water and slip the skins off.

Heat the olive oil in a deep frying pan over a moderate heat. Add the garlic and chilli and fry, without browning, for 20 seconds. Add the tomatoes and tomato paste and mix well. Bring to the boil and simmer for 1 minute. Add the bread, mix well and bring back to the boil. Stir in the basil. Taste and season with salt and freshly ground black pepper.

- *or* *simply serve the Pappa al Pomodoro by itself as a soup, as is traditional*
- *or* *make the Pappa al Pomodoro without the bread and simmer it until thick, make double the mussels and serve them with the pappa as a dipping sauce for a finger food to go with drinks*
- *or* *make a mixture of seafood instead of just using mussels – raw scallops and/or shelled prawns wrapped in prosciutto then barbecued are delicious alternatives.*

Mussels with Salami, Tomatoes and Lettuce

This was inspired by a Provençal recipe from the immortal Elizabeth David and is an aromatic dish of mussels cooked on slow-fried onions, garlic, salami and tomatoes with wine and lettuce. In old French recipes lettuce was often cooked. *Serves 6*

3 tablespoons olive oil

1 onion, finely chopped

3 cloves garlic, finely chopped

100g (3 1/2 oz) spicy salami, finely diced

400g (14oz) canned Italian tomatoes in juice, mashed

18 Greek black olives

36 live mussels, scrubbed, beards pulled out

1 small iceberg lettuce, thinly sliced

freshly ground black pepper

Heat the olive oil over a moderate heat in a large saucepan. Add the onion, garlic and salami and fry gently for about 10 minutes, until the onion is soft. Add the tomatoes and olives and mix well.

Add the mussels and cook until they have all opened, removing them to a warm bowl as they do. If you overcook them, they will be tough.

When all the mussels have been removed stir in the lettuce, bring to the boil and let the lettuce wilt. Taste the lettuce mixture – the mussels are salty so it won't need salt but season with freshly ground black pepper.

Serve the mussels on the lettuce and sauce with crusty bread on the side.

or *use chunks of firm white fish and some boiled waxy potato chunks instead of the mussels, but take care not to overcook the fish*

or *turn it into a main course by serving the mussels and lettuce mixture on rice*

or *instead of the mussels, panfry diced boneless chicken breast until browned, remove from the pan and proceed with the recipe, adding the browned chicken instead of the mussels, and finish as for the recipe.*

Mussels and Fish with Saffron Cream

Perfumed by the saffron, this is a small, rich dish which is perfect as a first course. *Serves 6*

2 tomatoes, cored, seeded and cut into
   1/2cm (1/4 in) dice
juice of 1 lime
24 live mussels, scrubbed, beards
   pulled out
125ml (4fl oz) water
3 tablespoons olive oil
3 cloves garlic, finely chopped
1 small dried red chilli, finely chopped
1 small onion, finely chopped
1 small carrot, finely diced
1/2 stick celery, finely diced
1/2 teaspoon saffron, toasted and
   powdered (see page 156)
400g (14oz) skinless, boneless firm white
   fish fillets, such as snapper, monkfish,
   blue cod, hapuku or groper, cut into
   3cm (1 1/4 in) dice
250ml (9fl oz) cream
flaky sea salt and freshly ground
   black pepper
12 thin slices cucumber
coriander leaves

Toss the tomatoes in half the lime juice.

Steam the mussels open in the water, remove the shells, strain, and reserve 125ml (4fl oz) of the liquid.

Heat the olive oil over a moderate heat, add the garlic, chilli, onion, carrot, celery and saffron and sauté, without browning, until the vegetables are soft.

Add the remaining lime juice, the mussels, fish and the mussel liquid and mix well. Add the cream, bring to the boil, and boil for 1 minute. Taste and season with salt and pepper.

Put four mussels in each of six warm plates with a little of the diced fish and cream sauce. Put two slices of cucumber on each portion and sprinkle each portion with some tomatoes and coriander leaves.

or *serve on rice for lunch with a green salad*
or *cut six small rectangles of ready-rolled flaky pastry, brush the tops with beaten egg, put them on a baking tray and bake at 200°C (400°F) until puffed and well browned, then split the pastries in half horizontally and serve the mussels and fish in the sauce between the pastry layers*
or *serve on plenty of spinach leaves which have been wilted in a hot pan with a little olive oil, salt and pepper.*

Sour Squid Salad

This has the sweet, sour, salty and hot flavours I love about the food of South-East Asia. It is an assembly of briefly cooked squid, melon and crunchy celery with the Vietnamese combination of lime juice, fish sauce, chilli and sugar. This is a delicious hot weather first course. *Serves 6*

5 squid tubes, opened out flat and very
   thinly sliced
4 tablespoons lime juice
4 tablespoons fish sauce
1 small fresh red chilli (or to taste),
   thinly sliced
2 tablespoons sugar
2 cloves garlic, finely chopped
1 tablespoon finely chopped
   coriander stalks
3 tablespoons sesame oil
1 large, firm green-fleshed Honeydew
   melon, peeled, seeded and thinly sliced
1 stick celery, thinly sliced on the diagonal
ready-to-use fried sliced shallots or fresh
   shallots and peanut oil
coriander leaves
lime wedges

Drop the sliced squid into boiling salted water for 2 minutes or until all the squid has turned white, remove and place under cold running water to cool. Drain well.

Put the lime juice, fish sauce, chilli, sugar, garlic and coriander stalks into a salad bowl and mix until the sugar has dissolved. Add the squid and toss well. Set aside for 15 minutes. Add the sesame oil, melon and celery and mix well.

If using fresh shallots, thinly slice and fry in hot peanut oil until crisp and golden brown. Drain well. Sprinkle the shallots and coriander leaves over the salad and serve with the lime wedges.

or *serve the salad on cellophane, bean thread or Lungkow noodles, soaked in hot water until soft, cooked in boiling water for a few minutes until transparent, then drained and cooled in cold water*

or *use thinly sliced skinned boneless chicken breast which has been poached in salted simmering water instead of squid*

or *toss some pork fillets in crushed garlic and peanut oil and barbecue until well browned and cooked through. Remove from the heat, let it rest, then thinly slice. Use hot instead of the squid, put everything on crisp lettuce leaves and sprinkle the salad with chopped roasted peanuts as well.*

Barbecued Squid and Chorizo Salad

Salads come in all shapes and sizes with a huge variety of possible ingredients. The common component in all salads is a dressing. The following dish is a warm salad with a chunky tomato dressing. Chorizos are available from most supermarkets. *Serves 6*

Dressing

*4 large ripe tomatoes, cored, seeded and
   finely chopped*
125ml (4fl oz) extra virgin olive oil
2 tablespoons lemon juice
1 clove garlic, finely chopped
1/2 small red onion, finely chopped
*2 tablespoons chopped coriander leaves
   and stalks*
*flaky sea salt and freshly ground
   black pepper*

Mix all the ingredients together, taste and check the seasoning, and set aside for 30 minutes.

Salad

4 whole squid tubes
*flaky sea salt and freshly ground
   black pepper*
2 large spicy chorizo sausages
olive oil
2 large handfuls rocket leaves
12 black olives

Open the tubes out flat and score the skin in a grid pattern. Season well with salt and pepper.

Brush the chorizos with olive oil and barbecue over a moderate heat until hot and browned. Remove and slice.

Wipe the barbecue clean of oil with paper towels, heat it until very hot and put the squid, scored side down, on the grill. Cook quickly just until they go white on each side and roll up. Remove from the barbecue and thinly slice the squid.

To serve, put the squid down the middle of a large platter. Sprinkle the sliced chorizo over the squid. Put the rocket and olives down each side. Spoon the dressing over everything.

*or add steamed white rice to turn the salad into
   a main course*
*or use barbecued salmon fillet instead of squid –
   barbecue the salmon in a large piece, then
   break it into bite-sized pieces and proceed
   with the salad*
*or brush some thinly sliced courgette or
   eggplant with olive oil, barbecue until golden,
   put the squid and chorizo on top of them and
   proceed with the salad.*

Salmon Tartare

Raw salmon has a mild, rich, creamy flavour that is an excellent foil for many other more strongly flavoured ingredients. This simple dish is one of my favourites. *Serves 6*

400g (14oz) very fresh skinless, boneless
*   salmon fillet, finely diced*
3 tablespoons capers
finely grated zest of 1 lemon
1/2 cucumber, peeled, seeded and
*   finely diced*
3 tablespoons chopped chervil
4 tablespoons extra virgin olive oil
flaky sea salt and freshly ground
*   black pepper*
finely diced flesh of 1 lemon
6 thin slices white sourdough bread

Mix the first six ingredients. Taste and season with salt and pepper.

Serve sprinkled with the diced lemon, with toasted sourdough bread on the side.

or *spread the salmon mixture onto hot flatbread and drizzle well with yoghurt mixed with chopped mint leaves, a finely chopped clove of garlic and salt to taste*

or *serve the cold salmon mixture on hot steamed rice in small bowls with light soy sauce on the side, and green salad to follow*

or *serve the salmon with warm chopped soft-boiled eggs and a little Tabasco sauce on salad greens, either as a first-course salad or lunch dish.*

Steamed Salmon and Leeks with Herbed Cream

A delicate herb-infused cream served over pale green steamed leeks and rosy pink salmon. Buying a bamboo steamer with two layers, big enough to accommodate a large dinner plate in each, was one of the best things I ever did. Steaming things like fish or shellfish seems to intensify their flavours. *Serves 6*

Herbed Cream
300ml (10 1/2 fl oz) cream
finely grated zest and juice of 1 lemon
1 tablespoon chopped fresh tarragon
1 tablespoon chopped dill
1/2 clove garlic, finely chopped
flaky sea salt and freshly ground
*   black pepper*

Put the cream, lemon juice and zest, herbs and garlic into a saucepan and bring to the boil. Simmer for 1 minute, taste and season with salt and pepper. Set aside and keep warm.

Salmon and Leeks
6 x 100g (3 1/2 oz) slices skinned, boned
*   salmon fillet*
flaky sea salt
3 leeks, ends trimmed, split lengthways
chervil sprigs for garnish

Lightly sprinkle the salmon with salt. Blanch the leeks by dropping into boiling water for 2 minutes, then refresh in cold water and drain well.

Make a layer of the strips of blanched leek on a dinner plate and place the salmon pieces on top. Put the plate into a steamer over a high heat and steam for 10 minutes or until the salmon is just cooked.

Remove the salmon and leeks to a large warm serving platter, spoon the Herbed Cream over everything, then sprinkle with plenty of fresh chervil sprigs.

or *follow the same recipe but use sliced boneless chicken breasts instead, allowing a little extra time for them to cook, and serve with rice for a light lunch*

or *follow the recipe but use scallops instead of salmon*

or *spoon the cream over oysters on the half shell which have been only just heated through but not overcooked on the plate in the steamer, or mussels which have been opened in a saucepan by bringing them to the boil and simmering with a little white wine.*

Salmon Carpaccio

Carpaccio is traditionally thin slices of raw beef and flavourings. Here the beef is replaced with thin slices of rich, creamy raw salmon with the appropriate flavourings added. This recipe came from a Tahitian friend and is a successful mix of European and Asian tastes. It makes a stunning first course when presented on a big white platter. *Serves 6*

*500g (1lb 2oz) skinless, boneless fresh
    salmon fillet*
extra virgin olive oil for sprinkling
2 tablespoons finely chopped ginger
finely grated zest of 2 limes
*2 tablespoons chopped coriander stalks
    and leaves*
flaky sea salt
lime wedges

Slice the salmon on the diagonal, as thinly as possible, slicing towards the tail end. Lie the salmon slices out flat to cover a large platter.

Sprinkle liberally with the olive oil. Scatter the ginger, lime zest and coriander over the top and season well with salt.

Garnish with the lime wedges but don't let the flesh of the limes come in contact with the salmon or it will lose its deep pink colour and turn milky.

Serve with crusty sourdough bread and a squeeze of lime juice as you eat.

or *sticking to the method, replace the ginger, lime and coriander with thinly sliced sundried tomatoes and sliced pitted black Greek olives, and put a big handful of rocket leaves on top in the centre*

or *replace the ginger, lime and coriander with sliced green olives, capers, thinly sliced spring onions, lemon zest and freshly ground black pepper*

or *make a layer of thinly sliced cucumber, lay the salmon on top, drizzle with plain yoghurt instead of oil and sprinkle with salt, pepper, mint and basil leaves.*

Hot-smoked Salmon Bruschetta with Tomato Chilli Conserve

Hot-smoking salmon is easy. It is really just salmon cooked in an enclosed space with smoke. *Serves 6*

Salmon
4 tablespoons brown sugar
extra virgin olive oil
600g (1lb 5oz) boned salmon fillet, cut
  into 6 equal pieces
natural wood chips

Mix the sugar with enough extra virgin olive oil to make a thick paste. Spread the sugar and oil paste over the flesh side of the salmon.

Line a wok with tin foil and put a small handful of natural wood chips in the bottom. Put the salmon on a rack in the wok, cover tightly with more foil, and place over a high heat until you can smell smoke. Turn the heat to medium and smoke for 8 minutes or until just cooked through. Remove the salmon from the wok, turn it onto a platter and peel off the skin.

Tomato Chilli Conserve
4 tablespoons olive oil
3 cloves garlic, finely chopped
1 small fresh red chilli, finely sliced
1 small onion, thinly sliced
1 red capsicum (pepper), cored, seeded and
  sliced
1 teaspoon sweet Spanish smoked paprika
400g (14oz) can Italian tomatoes in juice,
  mashed
1 tablespoon sugar
flaky sea salt and freshly ground
  black pepper

Heat the olive oil over a moderate heat and add all the ingredients except the tomatoes, sugar and seasoning. Fry gently until the onions are soft and transparent, but do not brown them.

Add the tomatoes and sugar, and season with salt and pepper. Simmer until thick. Set aside. *Makes about 500ml (18fl oz)*

Bruschetta
6 x 2cm (³⁄₄ in) thick slices of French bread
  or ciabatta
1 large clove garlic, peeled

Toast or barbecue the bread until golden on each side and rub with the garlic.

Garnish
1 bunch rocket leaves
extra virgin olive oil

To serve, put the bruschetta onto a platter, spread some Tomato Chilli Conserve onto each piece of Bruschetta and place a slice of salmon on top. Put the rocket leaves around everything and lightly sprinkle with olive oil.

or use the hot smoked salmon in a green salad as a first course
or serve the salmon with scrambled eggs for brunch
or use the Tomato Chilli Conserve with thinly sliced barbecued chicken breast and steamed rice as a main course and follow with a salad.

Tequila Snapper Ceviche

I love raw and marinated fish dishes. Many people shy away from fish prepared like this, as they think it will taste too strong. On the contrary, raw and marinated fish usually has a more delicate flavour than cooked.

In this ceviche, which is the South American name for this type of marinated raw fish dish, chunks of snapper are marinated until white, then drained and mixed with flavourings which make it almost like a tequila-based Bloody Mary salad. *Serves 6*

6 large tomatoes, cored, seeded
    and halved
250ml (9fl oz) fresh lemon or lime juice
600g (1lb 5oz) skinned, boned snapper
    fillet, cut into 3cm (1 1/4 in) pieces
1 red onion, finely chopped
1 clove garlic, finely chopped
24 pimento-stuffed olives
1/2 teaspoon sweet Spanish smoked
    paprika
4 tablespoons Tabasco sauce
3 tablespoons Worcestershire sauce
50ml (2fl oz) tequila
3 tablespoons extra virgin olive oil
4 tablespoons chopped flat-leafed parsley
1 red capsicum (pepper), cored, seeded
    and thinly sliced
flaky sea salt to taste
3 Hass avocados, peeled and cut into
    3cm (1 1/4 in) dice
lime wedges and parsley sprigs for garnish

Rub the tomatoes with a little olive oil and grill or barbecue until just collapsing, then skin and mash.

Mix the lemon juice and fish and set aside for 30 minutes, then drain and discard the juice.

Put the fish into a bowl, add all the ingredients except the avocados and garnish, and mix well. Set aside for 1 hour.

Add the avocados, mix carefully, and put everything onto a deep platter. Garnish with lime wedges and parsley.

or use halved raw scallops and shelled prawns instead of fish for a deluxe start to a special meal – serve with bought flour tortillas which you have heated in the oven until piping hot but still soft and tender

or serve the ceviche on salad greens and make it more like a salad

or panfry thinly sliced boneless chicken breast in some olive oil with a little chopped garlic, pepper and salt; omit the fish and lime juice and mix the hot chicken with everything else and serve with rice.

Steamed Seafood with Soba Noodles and Greens

The inspiration for this very elegant first course or lunch was a wonderful Japanese recipe by Shizuo Tsuji. I use a large bamboo Chinese steamer with two layers, which is very efficient. *Serves 6*

500ml (18fl oz) well-flavoured liquid
   fish stock
100ml (3 ½ fl oz) mirin
100ml (3 ½ fl oz) light Japanese soy sauce
15g (½oz) dried bonito flakes
150g (5oz) Japanese green tea
   soba noodles
1 sheet nori
300g (10 ½ oz) skinless, boneless firm
   white fish fillets
6 scallops
6 raw prawns
6 shucked oysters
180ml (6fl oz) sake
6 small spinach leaves
6 small bok choy leaves
2 spring onions, thinly sliced

Put the fish stock, mirin and soy sauce into a saucepan and bring to the boil. Add the bonito flakes and then strain immediately or the mixture will become bitter. Discard the bonito flakes and keep the sauce hot but not boiling.

Cook the noodles in plenty of boiling water until tender to the bite, cool under cold water and drain well.

Toast the nori by quickly sweeping it over a gas flame or hot electric element until you see it crinkle up a little, then cut into thin strips with scissors.

Cut the fish into six equal pieces. In six small bowls, teacups or ramekins, put a small mound of the noodles and a piece of each type of the seafood. Put a spinach and bok choy leaf, and a few slices of spring onion on top. Sprinkle the contents of each bowl with 2 tablespoons of sake.

Cover each bowl tightly with plastic food wrap and steam over a high heat for 15–20 minutes, until the seafood is cooked and the noodles hot.

Remove from the steamer, uncover, and top with the hot sauce. Sprinkle toasted nori strips on top and serve.

or use very thinly sliced chicken breast instead of seafood, but make sure it is well cooked
or spoon the sauce over a whole baked fish or baked side of salmon and serve with steamed rice and a green salad for a main course
or make a vegetarian version by substituting tofu for the seafood.

Steamed Fish with Roasted Tomatoes and Olives

The roasted tomatoes and olives turn into a delicious sauce for the lemony steamed fish. *Serves 6*

Sauce

*12 medium-sized vine-ripened tomatoes,
    cored, tops nicked in a cross shape*
24 stoned black Greek kalamata olives
2 cloves garlic, finely chopped
2 tablespoons extra virgin olive oil
*flaky sea salt and freshly ground
    black pepper*

Put everything into a roasting dish, mix well, turn the tomatoes so they are core side down and roast in the oven for 15 minutes or until well cooked. Remove from the oven and keep warm.

Fish

2 tablespoons extra virgin olive oil
*600g (1lb 5oz) skinless, boneless firm white
    fish fillets cut into 5cm (2in) pieces*
4 tablespoons dry vermouth
finely grated zest of 1 lemon
2 handfuls rocket leaves
1 small handful Italian parsley sprigs
*flaky sea salt and freshly ground
    black pepper*

Toss all the ingredients together and place in a shallow bowl. Put the bowl in a bamboo steamer over boiling water and steam for 5 minutes or until the fish is just cooked. Remove from the steamer.

Serve the fish on warm plates with the Tomato and Olive Sauce on top, with bread on the side.

or serve with couscous or rice as a main course
*or replace the fish with thinly sliced boneless
    chicken breast*
*or use the tomatoes and olives with bread as
    antipasto.*

Fish Baked 'en Papillote' with Green Olive Tapenade

This is a perfect first course for a special dinner or with salad for a special lunch. The aroma when the papillotes or paper packages are opened at the table is mouth-watering. The dish takes a little time, but it is only an assembly of vegetables, fish and herbs inside a package served with a salty green olive and almond paste.

If the idea of using folded paper for the fish is like an origami nightmare to you, use tin foil. Just fold over the edges and make sure they are sealed. It's not as pleasant to look at or eat from but just as efficient as the paper. *Serves 6*

Tapenade

20 pitted green olives
75g (3oz) roasted blanched almonds
1 small handful flat-leafed parsley leaves
1 clove garlic
2 tablespoons capers
125ml (4fl oz) extra virgin olive oil

Put all the ingredients into a food processor and process until you have a chunky paste. Put into a bowl and set aside.

Papillotes

4 large floury potatoes
1 large fennel bulb, cored and thinly sliced
18 cloves garlic, peeled
4 tablespoons extra virgin olive oil
6 x 30cm (12in) diameter circles of baking
*   paper*
6 boneless firm white fish fillets, skin on
*   (about 100g, 3 1/2 oz each)*
finely grated zest of 1 lemon
6 sprigs fresh thyme
flaky sea salt and freshly ground
*   black pepper*

Preheat the oven to 190°C (375°F). Peel the potatoes, slice 2cm (1in) thick, boil until tender, drain well and leave to steam dry.

Put the fennel, garlic and extra virgin olive oil into a roasting dish and toss well. Place in the oven and roast, turning occasionally, until soft and well browned, about 30 minutes. Remove from the oven and cool.

To make one papillote proceed as follows. On one side of a circle of paper put one-sixth of the potatoes, one-sixth of the fennel and 3 cloves of garlic. Put a fillet of fish on top. Sprinkle a little lemon zest on top and put a thyme sprig on top of that. Season with salt and pepper. Fold the paper in half so you have a semicircle and fold over twice in sections around the edge to close. Repeat to make the other five parcels.

Put the papillotes onto a baking tray and place in the oven. Bake for 35 minutes and remove from the oven.

Place each papillote on a plate and open at the table. Serve with a big dollop of the tapenade.

or *serve the tapenade by itself as a dip with warm flatbread with drinks or as an accompaniment for barbecued chicken*

or *dispense with the paper cases and layer the cooked fennel and garlic, sliced potatoes, fish and herbs in an oven dish, moisten with a little white wine and bake until cooked*

or *do the same thing in the oven dish but use thinly sliced chicken breast instead of fish.*

Fishcakes with Hot Sour Broth and Cellophane Noodles

Not just a soup, this has panfried fishcakes, made the Asian way, using only fish and flavourings. *Serves 6*

Fishcakes

*500g (1lb 2oz) skinless, boneless firm
    white fish fillets, such as monkfish,
    gurnard, hapuku, snapper, tarakihi*
1 spring onion, chopped
125ml (4fl oz) canned coconut cream
2 cloves garlic, chopped
1 tablespoon chopped ginger
1 egg white
1 teaspoon flaky sea salt

Put all the ingredients into a food processor and process until smooth. Fry tablespoonfuls in a little hot peanut oil for about 3 minutes each side until golden. Keep warm. *Makes 18*

Noodles and Broth

*150g (5oz) cellophane, bean thread or
    Lungkow noodles*
*750ml (27fl oz) well-flavoured liquid
    chicken stock*
2 kaffir lime leaves
1/2 teaspoon finely ground turmeric
2 cloves garlic, finely chopped
1 teaspoon coriander root, finely chopped
*1 small fresh red chilli (or more to taste),
    finely sliced*
2 tablespoons fish sauce
1 tablespoon finely grated palm sugar
50ml (2fl oz) lime juice
coriander and mint leaves for garnish

Soak the noodles until soft in hot water.

Put the remaining ingredients except the garnish into a saucepan and bring to the boil. Simmer for 2 minutes and add the drained noodles. Bring back to the boil and simmer for 3 minutes.

Serve the noodles at the bottom of large soup bowls with the fishcakes on top and with everything moistened with the broth.

or *use the fishcakes in a salad of thinly sliced
    cucumbers, tomatoes, red onions, and greens
    as a first course*
or *omit the fishcakes and use the broth to poach
    sliced fish, prawns and mussels or any
    combination of seafood, and serve it on the
    noodles with the broth*
or *add 250ml (9fl oz) coconut cream to the broth
    after it is cooked for a richer creamy broth.*

Pasta with Mascarpone and Walnuts

This is based on another Elizabeth David idea, this time an Italian one. It's not one for dieters, but it is staggeringly simple and extremely delicious as a first course or lunch followed by a green salad. *Serves 6*

500g (1lb 2oz) rigatoni or any ridged, short tubular pasta
250g (8 3/4 oz) mascarpone
finely grated zest of 1 lemon
150g (5oz) toasted walnut pieces
150g (5oz) finely grated good quality parmesan cheese
flaky sea salt and freshly ground black pepper to taste

Cook the pasta in plenty of boiling, well-salted water until al dente. Drain it and put it back into the hot saucepan over a low heat.

Add the other ingredients and gently toss until the cheeses are melted and hot but not boiling. Taste and season with salt and pepper.

Serve immediately on hot plates.

or *add a little chopped prosciutto and chives for a tasty alternative*

or *replace half the mascarpone with gorgonzola for an even richer dish*

or *add a few chopped sage leaves and let them wilt in the hot pasta when the other ingredients are added.*

Pasta with Tuna, Olives and Rocket

Canned tuna is an underrated ingredient which deserves a place in every cook's storecupboard. If you can get the Italian or Spanish white tuna in olive oil, this will make this recipe more luxurious.

This dish's success relies on taking time to slowly cook the onions. Once this is done, the other ingredients are quickly added, cooked and served on the hot pasta. *Serves 6*

500g (1lb 2oz) short tubular Italian pasta such as penne
flaky sea salt
4 tablespoons extra virgin olive oil
3 red onions, finely chopped
3 cloves garlic, finely chopped
juice of ½ lemon
zest of 1 lemon
3 anchovy fillets, chopped
125ml (4fl oz) dry white wine
18 pitted black olives
250g (8 ¾ oz) canned tuna in oil, drained and crumbled
1 large handful rocket leaves
freshly grated good quality parmesan cheese

Time the pasta to be ready when the sauce is ready. Cook the pasta in plenty of well-salted water until al dente and drain well.

Heat the olive oil over a moderate heat and add the onions, garlic, lemon juice and zest and anchovies. Mix well and fry gently, without browning, until the juice evaporates and the onions are soft.

Turn the heat up, add the wine and bring to the boil. Add the olives, tuna and rocket and cook, stirring, until everything is hot and the rocket is wilted.

Serve immediately on the pasta with plenty of freshly grated parmesan cheese.

or *use 5 chopped rashers of rindless bacon instead of the tuna – add the bacon with the onions and fry as directed*
or *crumble some feta over the dish instead of the parmesan cheese*
or *add 3–4 chopped tomatoes with the rocket.*

Tortillitas de Camarones

Another favourite from Spain, which I first ate in Seville. These tortillitas are excellent served with drinks or with lemon wedges as a first course. They are simply little fritters of chopped prawns fried in a batter of chickpea flour and flavourings. *Makes about 12*

1 spring onion, finely sliced
1 clove garlic, finely chopped
100g (5oz) plain flour
100g (5oz) chickpea flour
200g (7oz) shelled raw prawns, chopped
½ teaspoon flaky sea salt
1 tablespoon chopped flat-leafed parsley
about 250ml (9fl oz) water
olive oil for frying

Put all the ingredients except the olive oil into a bowl and mix with enough water to make a pouring batter.

Fry small spoonfuls in hot olive oil until crisp and golden on each side. Drain on paper towels.

or *use chopped fish or sliced cooked mussels instead of prawns*

or *make them into small one-bite fritters and serve with drinks before dinner*

or *add a teaspoon of toasted cumin seeds and another clove of finely chopped garlic to the batter, leave out the prawns and dip thin slices of kumara (sweet potato) or pumpkin, cauliflower or broccoli florets, thinly sliced eggplant or courgettes in the batter and fry in hot olive oil, then serve well drained with spicy chutney and plain yoghurt.*

Courgette and Almond Fritters with Greek Yoghurt

These delicate little fritters with tangy, sour Greek yoghurt are great as a first course. *Makes about 18*

9 small courgettes (zucchini), grated
1/2 teaspoon flaky sea salt
3 cloves garlic, finely chopped
finely grated zest of 1 lemon
50g (2oz) roasted almonds, chopped
6 tablespoons plain flour
1 egg, beaten
3 tablespoons chopped flat-leafed parsley
olive oil for frying
250ml (9fl oz) thick Greek yoghurt

Put the courgettes, salt, garlic, lemon zest and almonds into a mixing bowl and mix well. Set aside for 20 minutes for the salt to draw the juices out of the courgettes.

Add the flour, egg and parsley to the bowl and mix everything together to form a batter.

Fry spoonfuls in a little hot olive oil until well browned, turning to brown the other side.

Serve with a spoonful of Greek yoghurt.

or *serve without the yoghurt as an accompaniment to fried fish, roasted or panfried chicken or lamb*

or *instead of courgettes make the fritters with grated pumpkin, potato or carrots*

or *add a handful of chopped raw prawns to the mixture for a delicious variation*

or *try a spicy chutney with the fritters instead of Greek yoghurt.*

Pumpkin and Kumara Fritters with Avocado and Lime

It is hard to imagine how this mixture will cook in the seemingly brief time it spends in the frying pan, but it does – the outside of the fritters are crisp and brown and the inside almost steamed.

These little fritters are good with drinks, as a first course or for brunch. *Makes about 18*

300g (10 ½ oz) grated, peeled, seeded pumpkin

300g (10 ½ oz) grated, peeled kumara (sweet potato)

2 eggs, beaten

2 cloves garlic, finely chopped

2 tablespoons plain flour

2 tablespoons chopped coriander

flaky sea salt and freshly ground black pepper

olive oil for frying

3 firm Hass avocados, peeled, stoned and sliced

3 limes, halved

Put all the ingredients, except the olive oil, avocados and limes, in a bowl and mix well, seasoning well with salt and pepper.

Heat a little olive oil in a large frying pan over a moderate heat and fry large tablespoonfuls of the mixture until well browned on the underside, then turn and fry until well browned on the other side. Repeat until all of the mix is used. Keep warm on paper towels in a hot oven.

Serve with slices of avocado and half a lime for squeezing. Also good with Tabasco or chilli sauce.

or *stir 3 diced rindless rashers of bacon into the mix before frying*

or *stir 150g (5oz) crumbled feta into the mix before frying*

or *use grated floury potatoes instead of the pumpkin or kumara or both.*

Dhal Fritters with Masala Dipping Sauce

This is a version of a recipe that I developed for use as an appetiser when I was a restaurant chef.

Though you do need to think ahead and soak the dhal overnight, these delicious fritters are just spoonfuls of batter made of puréed dhal with flavouring, peas and onion fried in hot oil, with a spicy sweet and sour dipping sauce. Dhal, chickpea flour and palm sugar are available from Asian food shops. *Serves 6*

Fritters

300g (10 1/2 oz) chana dhal (or yellow split peas)
2 tablespoons finely chopped ginger
4 cloves garlic, finely chopped
1 large fresh green chilli, finely sliced
1 teaspoon flaky sea salt
1 tablespoon ground turmeric
200ml (7fl oz) canned coconut cream
1/2 teaspoon baking soda
5 tablespoons chickpea flour (besan)
1 handful frozen peas
1 handful coriander leaves, chopped
1 small onion, finely chopped
vegetable oil for frying

Soak the dhal overnight in plenty of cold water, then drain well.

Put all the ingredients except the peas, coriander, onion and vegetable oil into a food processor and process to a thick, smooth batter. Stir in the remaining ingredients.

Fry small spoonfuls on each side in hot vegetable oil until crisp and browned. Drain on paper towels.

Dipping Sauce

2 teaspoons cumin seeds
1/2 teaspoon fennel seeds
1/4 teaspoon fenugreek seeds
3 large fresh red chillies, seeded
6 shallots, peeled
4 cloves garlic
150g palm sugar, chopped
200ml lime juice
flaky sea salt to taste

Separately toast the seeds in a dry pan until they are fragrant and slightly darkened in colour. Grind the seeds or pound in a mortar until coarsely powdered.

Put the ground seeds and the other ingredients except the salt into a food processor and process until smooth and the sugar dissolved. Taste and season with salt. Pour into a bowl.

Serve the fritters with the sauce on the side. Good with drinks.

or stir 1 finely diced boneless single chicken breast into the fritter mix with the peas, onions and coriander

or make a hot lamb salad by panfrying or barbecuing 4 lamb shortloins, remove from the heat, let it rest, thinly slice and place the warm lamb onto your favourite salad greens, with the dipping sauce spooned over everything as the dressing

or use the fritters as an accompaniment to roast chicken, lamb or panfried steak.

Tomato, Fennel and Anchovy Salad

An Italian way of making a tomato salad is to salt the tomatoes first so that the acidic juice is released, making the addition of vinegar or lemon juice unnecessary.

As this is a simple recipe, it relies on good ingredients – there's no point making it if you have tasteless tomatoes. I like using the plump, mild-tasting, rose-coloured Spanish anchovies in this salad.

Good as a first course or as an accompaniment to a roast chicken or fried fish. *Serves 6*

*10 vine-ripened tomatoes, cut into
  bite-sized chunks*
¼ teaspoon flaky sea salt
freshly ground black pepper
50ml (2fl oz) extra virgin olive oil
1 red onion, thinly sliced
1 small clove garlic, finely chopped
12 black olives
*1 small bulb fresh fennel, sliced in half,
  cored, and thinly sliced*
10 anchovy fillets, drained
*3 slices toasted sourdough bread, torn into
  bite-sized pieces*
1 handful fresh basil leaves

Put all the ingredients except the fennel, anchovies, bread and basil into a salad bowl. Mix well and set aside for 30 minutes until the juices have run from the tomatoes.

Add the remaining ingredients and mix well.

or *add a handful of prawns briefly cooked in boiling salted water, leftover roast chicken, flaked smoked fish or sliced mozzarella for a more luxurious salad*

or *add some crumbled feta and a diced cucumber and turn it into a Greek-style village salad.*

Barbecued Chicken and Eggplant Salad

A simple assembly of hot smoky barbecued chicken, capsicum and eggplant with a tangy dressing. It is vital to use a good-quality Spanish paprika. *Serves 6*

3 single chicken breasts, sliced 2cm (1in) thick across the grain
3 tablespoons olive oil, plus extra for brushing
1 tablespoon sweet Spanish smoked paprika
2 cloves garlic, crushed to a paste
2 medium-sized eggplants (aubergines), sliced 1cm (1/2 in) thick
1 red capsicum (pepper), cored, seeded and quartered
flaky sea salt and freshly ground black pepper
1/2 cucumber, peeled, seeded and cut into 1cm (1/2 in) dice
12 black olives
finely grated zest of 1 lemon
2 large lemons, peeled and thinly sliced around the core
extra virgin olive oil for drizzling
2 tablespoons chopped flat-leafed parsley

Put the chicken breasts, 3 tablespoons of olive oil, paprika and garlic into a bowl and mix well.

Brush the eggplant slices and capsicum quarters with olive oil and season with salt and pepper. Grill the chicken, eggplant and capsicum on a hot barbecue until cooked and well browned.

Thinly slice the capsicum. Pile the eggplant and chicken onto a platter. Put the remaining ingredients on top, drizzle well with the olive oil and sprinkle the parsley on last.

or *panfry the chicken and bake the eggplant until golden on a baking tray in a hot oven*
or *use lamb shortloins or racks instead of chicken*
or *use thick, skinless, boneless firm white fish fillets instead of chicken.*

Grilled Eggplant and Courgette Salad

This is one of the simplest Italian-style salads and one which always pleases. An elegant first course. *Serves 6*

2 medium-sized eggplants (aubergines), sliced 1cm (1/2 in) thick
3 courgettes (zucchini), sliced 1cm (1/2 in) thick on the diagonal
extra virgin olive oil for brushing
flaky sea salt and freshly ground black pepper
1 small clove garlic, finely chopped
red wine vinegar
1 small handful mint leaves

Brush the eggplant and courgette slices with plenty of olive oil, season well with salt and pepper, and grill, barbecue or roast on trays in a hot oven until well browned.

Place the eggplant, courgettes and garlic in a wide bowl and sprinkle with a little vinegar. Scatter the mint leaves on top and serve.

or *turn into a main course by adding panfried chicken breast or barbecued eye-fillet of beef, cooked in one piece then thinly sliced*

or *serve sprinkled with crumbled goat's cheese or feta*

or *use the salad with panfried lamb racks or sliced shortloins, halved cherry tomatoes and olives.*

Skirt Steak Salad with Garlic Bruschetta

This is one of my favourite salads – it is good as a first course or as a meal by itself.

Skirt steak has an intensely delicious beef flavour. As with many cheap cuts of meat, you either fry it very hot and fast or very slowly on a low heat in a stew. Anything in between will result in it being tough.

Bruschetta is the traditional Roman version of garlic bread. *Serves 6*

Dressing

100ml (3 1/2 oz) olive oil

juice and zest of 1 lemon

1 clove garlic, finely chopped

3 gherkins, finely diced

2 tablespoons capers

2 hard-boiled eggs, finely chopped

*flaky sea salt and freshly ground
   black pepper*

Mix all the ingredients together, seasoning well with salt and pepper. Set aside.

Salad

2 cloves garlic, finely chopped

1/2 teaspoon cracked black pepper

1 tablespoon sumac

3 tablespoons olive oil

*600g beef skirt steak, in 1 piece, all fat and
   sinew removed*

1 small iceberg lettuce, cut into 6 wedges

4 tomatoes, cut into wedges

1 handful flat-leafed parsley sprigs

Mix the garlic, pepper, sumac and olive oil and rub it all over the steak. Set aside.

Put the lettuce, tomatoes and parsley onto a deep serving platter.

Heat a frying pan or barbecue grill until very hot and panfry or barbecue the steak for 3–4 minutes on each side, depending on how rare you like it. Remove from the heat and let it rest for 5 minutes in a warm place. Thinly slice the steak across the grain of the meat.

Put the sliced steak on top of the salad, and spoon the dressing over the top.

Serve with 2cm (3/4 in) thick slices of toasted white sourdough bread which have been rubbed with a cut clove of garlic while still hot, drizzled with olive oil and seasoned with salt and freshly ground black pepper.

or *serve the dressing over hot asparagus and slices of prosciutto as a first course*

or *use boneless chicken breasts or thighs instead of steak – the chicken needs to be cooked thoroughly so it will take longer at a lower temperature than the rare steak*

or *use this dressing on a poached fillet of beef for a main course. Poach a 700g (1lb 13oz) piece of eye-fillet of beef (all fat and sinew removed) in simmering beef stock that has some sliced onion, carrot, celery and a clove of garlic in it. This should take about 10 minutes for medium rare. Remove from the stock and let it rest in a warm place for 10 minutes. Thinly slice and serve with the dressing spooned over it and with plain potatoes and a green salad on the side.*

Yakitori

My version of the Japanese sweet soy and sake marinated chicken skewers. I have not used chicken livers, which are part of the traditional dish. The sake marinade can be used in many ways. *Serves 6*

75ml (3fl oz) sake
75ml (3fl oz) mirin
75ml (3fl oz) Japanese soy sauce
12 bamboo skewers
3 whole, skinless, boneless chicken breasts
6 spring onions

Mix the sake, mirin and soy sauce together.

Soak the bamboo skewers in water for 1 hour, then drain.

Cut the chicken breasts into 2.5cm (1in) cubes, to make 48 cubes of chicken. Cut the spring onion into 3cm (1 1/4 in) pieces, to make 36 pieces of spring onion. Thread four pieces of chicken alternately with three pieces of spring onion on each skewer.

Put the skewers in one layer in a wide, shallow container just big enough to hold them. Pour the sake mixture over the top and marinate for 2 hours, turning occasionally. Remove from the marinade and drain well. Reserve the marinade.

Heat a barbecue or grill until hot and grill or barbecue the skewers until cooked, turning them frequently. This should take about 10 minutes. Frequently brush the skewers with the extra marinade as they cook.

Serve two skewers per person. A small bowl of plain steamed white short grain Japanese rice each is an optional extra.

or use the sake marinade for large mushrooms, salmon fillet or beef steak – just barbecue or grill and brush frequently as they cook
or for a great main course, put a whole chicken in an ovenproof casserole, pour the sake marinade over the top, cover and roast in a hot oven until well cooked, then uncover, skim off the fat and serve with rice and stirfried bok choy
or for a vegetarian option, bake cubes of peeled, seeded pumpkin and tofu in a closed casserole with the marinade, and serve with rice and very fresh mung bean sprouts.

Sautéed Greens with Spice Paste

Two simple recipes put together to make a delicious first course or tapas. Spanish smoked paprika is very different from ordinary paprika and has a delightful smoky aroma and flavour. *Serves 6*

Spice Paste

3 vine-ripened tomatoes, cored
olive oil
1 red capsicum (pepper)
2 tablespoons each cumin and
    coriander seeds
75g (3oz) roasted almonds, chopped
3 cloves garlic, chopped
1 teaspoon sweet Spanish smoked paprika
2 small dried red chillies, finely chopped
flaky sea salt to taste

Greens

6 large leaves silverbeet (Swiss chard)
4 tablespoons extra virgin olive oil
3 cloves garlic, finely chopped
2 handfuls spinach leaves
2 handfuls rocket leaves
4 spring onions, sliced
flaky sea salt and freshly ground
    black pepper
flatbread or pita bread for serving

Rub the tomatoes with olive oil and roast in a 225°C (425°F) oven until browned and collapsing. Roast the capsicum separately in a hot oven until the skin blisters or over a gas flame until blackened, then skin, core and seed.

Toast the cumin and coriander seeds separately in a dry frying pan until they are fragrant and slightly darkened in colour.

Put all the ingredients except the salt into a food processor or blender and process until smooth. Taste and season with salt. Pour into a bowl and reserve.

Remove and discard the thick stems from the silverbeet and cook the leaves in boiling water until tender. Drain well, cool, squeeze dry and then chop.

Heat the olive oil over a moderate heat, add the garlic, fry for 10 seconds then add the silverbeet, spinach, rocket and spring onions. Turn up the heat and sauté everything until hot and well wilted. Season well with salt and pepper.

Serve the greens with a spoonful of the Spice Paste and warmed flatbread on the side.

or *use the greens as an accompaniment to roast chicken or lamb, steak or fried fish*

or *use the Spice Paste as a sauce – it is reminiscent of the Spanish sauce, Romesco, and is good with all sorts of plainly cooked food, such as poached or roast chicken, roast lamb, fried fish, plainly cooked potatoes or rice*

or *serve the Spice Paste as a dip for warm flatbread or raw vegetables.*

Pork and Chicken Liver Terrine

Most recipes for terrines make more than you need. This is a small recipe for a French-style terrine which is perfect for the first course of a special dinner or for lunch with bread and salad.

Don't be afraid of making a terrine – it is just a particularly delicious meatloaf which needs to be made in advance. *Serves 6–8*

3 cloves garlic, finely chopped
1 small red onion, finely chopped
2 teaspoons sugar
½ teaspoon flaky sea salt
½ teaspoon cracked black pepper
125ml (4fl oz) white wine
1 tablespoon fresh thyme leaves
finely grated zest of 1 lemon
2 single skinless and boneless chicken
*   breasts, sliced lengthways into*
*   2cm (¾ in) thick strips*
4 whole chicken livers, halved, all fat and
*   sinew removed*
250g (8 ¾ oz) minced belly pork
8 rashers rindless streaky bacon
2 fresh bay leaves

Mix all the ingredients together, except the bacon and the bay leaves, and marinate overnight.

Preheat the oven to 180°C (350°F). Line an 800ml (28fl oz) capacity terrine or loaf tin with the bacon, leaving some for the top.

Put the mixture into the tin, making sure that everything is distributed evenly and the chicken strips are lying lengthways down the tin. Cover the top with a layer of bacon and put the bay leaves on top. Cover with tin foil and bake in a large roasting dish half full of hot water for 1 hour or until the terrine is floating in its own juices.

Remove the terrine from the oven and from the roasting dish, but leave it in its tin. Press lightly until cold by balancing a plate on top of the terrine and putting a weight on top (full cans of fruit or vegetables make good weights). Do not use a heavy weight or you will squeeze all the juices out of the terrine and it will be dry. You just want to compress it slightly as it cools. Cover and refrigerate overnight.

Next day remove the terrine from its tin, slice and serve with little gherkins and crusty bread.

or put a line of pitted prunes down the middle of
*   the terrine before cooking*
or omit the chicken livers if desired and add
*   another single chicken breast*
or add a handful of shelled pistachios to the mix
*   before cooking.*

Peperoni alla Piemontese

This is a traditional North Italian antipasto – capsicums filled with garlic, tomatoes and anchovies, baked so that everything melts together. *Serves 6*

*6 red or yellow capsicums (peppers), cored,
    cut into quarters lengthways*
24 anchovy fillets
*4 vine-ripened tomatoes, cored and cut
    into thin wedges*
6 cloves garlic, very thinly sliced
200ml (7fl oz) extra virgin olive oil
freshly ground black pepper

Preheat the oven to 200°C (400°F).

Put the capsicum quarters into an oiled roasting dish in one layer, skin side down. Into each piece put 1 anchovy fillet, 1 tomato wedge, some garlic slices and 1–2 teaspoons olive oil. Sprinkle with black pepper.

Bake for 15–20 minutes until well browned but not collapsing – the capsicums should still have a slight crunch. Remove from the oven and cool.

Serve with ciabatta or other white sourdough bread as a first course.

or *serve the capsicums as an accompaniment to panfried steak with a green salad on the side as a main course*

or *place each filled raw capsicum quarter in a square of flaky pastry, diagonally pull two of the corners of the pastry together, brush the pastry with beaten egg then bake until the capsicum is browned and the pastry well cooked, puffed and golden*

or *dribble a little cream over everything and bake – this results in a sauce like the famous Piemontese dish, bagna cauda.*

Homemade Ricotta Antipasto

Ricotta is traditionally made from the whey left over after mozzarella is made. This 'ricotta' consists of fresh curds which have a delicious sweet cooked-milk flavour and are excellent presented on an antipasto platter.

The milk is simply heated then coagulated into curds by the reaction of the acid in the lemon juice with the milk protein. *Serves 6*

Homemade Ricotta
1 litre (35fl oz) full cream milk
125ml (4fl oz) cream
juice of 1 lemon
extra virgin olive oil for drizzling
1 clove garlic, finely chopped
flaky sea salt and freshly ground
  black pepper
finely grated zest of 1 lemon

Bring the milk and cream to the boil, remove from the heat and squeeze in the lemon juice. The mixture will separate and form curds and whey. Let it stand for 5 minutes.

Gently pour everything into a muslin-lined sieve and let the curds drain for about 30 minutes until cool and solid but not tough and hard. Discard the whey.

Turn the ricotta out onto a platter. It will stay in the shape in which it drained and have the pattern of the cloth on it. Drizzle well with the olive oil. Sprinkle the garlic, salt, black pepper and lemon zest on top.

Accompaniments
broad beans
thinly sliced radishes
caper berries or capers
black and green olives
sliced sundried or semidried tomatoes

Drop the broad beans into boiling water for 4 minutes, drain, cool under running cold water and then shell.

Surround the ricotta with small piles of the accompaniments. Serve slices of a chewy white sourdough bread separately.

or *crumble the ricotta over the greens when making the Sautéed Greens with Spice Paste recipe on page 58*

or *mix the ricotta into a stuffing for a whole roast chicken – make the stuffing from fresh breadcrumbs, the ricotta, finely chopped garlic, fresh thyme leaves, finely grated lemon zest, salt and freshly ground black pepper*

or *fry some well-seasoned onions, chopped bacon and plenty of garlic, and toss with hot spaghetti, the crumbled ricotta, stoned black olives and finely grated parmesan cheese, and serve as a first course or for lunch.*

Judith's Tostadas with Lemon Mayonnaise and Various Toppings

This is a recipe from an old friend, who has often served these tostadas to me as a first course. Tostada just means 'toast', one of my favourite foods.

The choice of bread is important. Choose a white sourdough loaf that when toasted has an appetising chewy texture and a crunchy crust. *Serves 6*

Mayonnaise

Mayonnaise is an emulsion that will only work if you take time to literally add the oil drop by drop in the beginning. It can easily be made in a food processor. If it curdles and will not thicken, pour the curdled mixture into a bowl. Wash and dry the food processor, put another egg yolk into the processor and start again with more oil, adding it slowly until you see it thicken and become creamy. Once this has happened, you can then add the curdled mixture slowly until everything is thick and unctuous.

3 egg yolks
finely grated zest of 1 lemon
300ml (10 1/2 fl oz) light olive or safflower oil
flaky sea salt and freshly ground
*   black pepper*
lemon juice to taste

Beat the yolks and lemon zest and add the oil drop by drop until it thickens. Continue adding the oil in a thin stream until fully incorporated. Season with salt, pepper and lemon juice. Set aside.

Tostadas
12 slices white sourdough bread, toasted on
*   each side and spread thickly with the*
*   mayonnaise*
12 shelled, butterflied fresh prawns, tossed
*   in a little olive oil, finely chopped garlic*
*   and a pinch of ground red chillies*
12 canned artichoke hearts, tossed in a little
*   olive oil and 1 tablespoon wholegrain*
*   mustard*
3 large portobello mushrooms, tossed in
*   finely chopped garlic, fresh tarragon*
*   leaves and a little olive oil*
12 shelled oysters, drained and tossed in
*   plain flour*
olive oil for frying

Separately barbecue or panfry the prawns, artichoke heart halves, mushrooms and oysters until everything is browned and the mushrooms are soft. Do not overcook the oysters, they just need to be browned in a little hot olive oil.

To serve, pile four prawns onto each of three tostadas. Slice the artichoke hearts thickly and pile them onto each of three tostadas. Thinly slice the mushrooms and pile onto each of three tostadas. Put four oysters onto each of the remaining three tostadas. Slice the tostadas in half. Put everything onto a large platter and serve. Good with a green salad as lunch or a light meal.

or *use any combination of the above toppings or just one of them, don't change the toast and mayonnaise part*

or *add 1–2 crushed cloves of garlic to the mayonnaise and serve with sliced smoked fish roe and raw vegetables such as thinly sliced fennel, carrots, celery, cucumber and tomatoes, with bread on the side*

or *dispense with the bread and serve the toppings on salad greens as a salad with the mayonnaise in a bowl on the side.*

Quick Sesame Bread with Barbecued Eggplant Pickle

This is an easy no-knead bread which is great by itself or with just about anything. It is reminiscent of Turkish bread, and is like a scone dough but risen with yeast. Make sure the milk and water are lukewarm or blood heat, which means they are as warm as you are. If the liquid is too hot, it will kill the yeast; if it is too cold, the yeast will not activate. *Serves 6*

Sesame Bread
1 teaspoon dried yeast
250ml (9fl oz) lukewarm milk
250ml (9fl oz) lukewarm water
2 teaspoons extra virgin olive oil
2 tablespoons honey
500g (1lb 2oz) plain flour
1/2 teaspoon flaky sea salt
2 tablespoons sesame seeds, plus extra
 for sprinkling
1 egg yolk beaten with a little milk

Eggplant Pickle
2 eggplants (aubergines), sliced into 1cm
 (1/2 in) thick slices
extra virgin olive oil for brushing and
 drizzling
flaky sea salt and freshly ground
 black pepper
100ml (3 1/2 fl oz) white wine vinegar
finely grated zest of 1 lemon
2 cloves garlic, finely chopped
1 handful each basil and mint leaves

Mix the yeast with the milk and water and set aside for 5 minutes. The yeast will melt into the liquid. Stir well to make sure there are no lumps.

Put the olive oil, honey, flour, salt and sesame seeds into a warm bowl.

Add the yeast mixture and mix well (I use my hands and squeeze the mixture to mix in the honey) until everything is evenly incorporated. Set aside in a clean bowl in a warm place to rise until doubled in bulk.

Preheat the oven to 220°C (425°F).

Punch down the dough and divide into six equal portions. Knead each briefly and roll out each on a lightly floured surface into a circle about 20cm (8in) in diameter. Fold each in half so that you have six semicircular shapes.

Place on oiled baking trays, brush with the egg mixture and sprinkle with sesame seeds. Put in a warm place until risen again by half.

Stipple the tops by pressing all over with oiled fingertips and bake for 15 minutes or until well cooked. Remove from the oven, wrap in a clean cloth and keep warm, or cool and reheat.

Brush the eggplant slices with some olive oil and barbecue over a moderate heat until well browned. Layer the eggplant slices into a small bowl, sprinkling salt, pepper, olive oil, vinegar, lemon zest, garlic and herbs between each layer. Set aside for 30 minutes.

Serve the pickle with the warm bread.

or *use the bread and pickle as part of an antipasto platter – add some thinly sliced salami, olives, artichoke hearts and cherry tomatoes, keeping everything in separate piles on the platter*

or *for a deluxe hot chicken salad, line a platter with salad greens, barbecue some well-seasoned boneless chicken breasts, slice them, serve on the greens with the pickle on top and warm bread on the side*

or *barbecue some lamb shortloins tossed in crushed garlic and olive oil, and once cooked, thinly slice, split the breads and stuff them with the lamb, the pickle, a little hummus and some rocket leaves – serve for lunch.*

large plates

These dishes are often a mix of easy recipes put together to create a substantial dish, and any of them could be the focus of a special meal comprising several courses, or a one-course everyday meal for the family.

Tagine of Fish on Couscous with Slow-cooked Vegetables

This is an economical recipe because it works well with any of the cheaper types of firm fish, such as gurnard, tarakihi, lemon fish or skate wings. *Serves 6*

Couscous

3 tablespoons olive oil
2 onions, thinly sliced
1 medium-sized kumara (sweet potato), peeled and cut into 2cm (1in) dice
200g (7oz) peeled, seeded pumpkin, cut into 2cm (1in) dice
250g (9oz) French instant couscous
boiling water
flaky sea salt and freshly ground black pepper

Heat the olive oil in a frying pan over a moderate heat and add the onions, kumara and pumpkin. When everything is hot and beginning to fry, turn the heat down low, cover, and cook slowly, stirring occasionally, until the vegetables are tender, about 15 minutes.

Meanwhile put the couscous into a heatproof bowl and add enough boiling water to cover. Quickly mix well and cover tightly. Set aside for 20 minutes. Uncover and fluff up with a fork so that there are no lumps. The couscous will still be hot.

Gently mix the vegetables and couscous and season well with salt and pepper.

Tagine

½ teaspoon ground turmeric
½ teaspoon flaky sea salt
juice of 1 lemon
700g (1lb 9oz) skinned, boned fish fillets, cut into 5cm (2in) chunks
3 tablespoons olive oil
1 onion, finely chopped
2 cloves garlic, finely chopped
1 tablespoon cumin seeds
finely grated zest of 1 lemon
1 carrot, finely diced
2 tablespoons sultanas
375ml (13fl oz) well-flavoured liquid chicken stock
250ml (9fl oz) water
flaky sea salt and freshly ground black pepper to taste
3 tablespoons chopped coriander

Mix the turmeric, salt and lemon juice and brush all over the fish. Set aside for 20 minutes.

Heat the olive oil in a deep frying pan over a moderate heat, add the fish in batches and fry on each side until starting to brown. Remove to a plate and set aside. Add the onion, garlic, cumin, lemon zest, carrot and sultanas to the pan. Fry gently, without browning, until the onion is soft.

Add the stock and water, bring to the boil and simmer for 5 minutes. Add the fish and simmer until it is just cooked through. Be careful not to overcook. Taste and season. Sprinkle the chopped coriander on top.

Serve the fish on the couscous.

or *use diced chicken instead of fish*
or *serve the couscous with roast lamb or chicken.*

Tuna with Salmorejo and White Beans and Mint

Salmorejo is an uncooked chilled gazpacho soup from Cordoba in Spain, which is thick because it doesn't have water in it. It is made in a food processor and makes an excellent (but untraditionally Spanish) sauce for panfried tuna.

Cook the tuna medium rare so that it retains its beautiful rich, creamy texture and flavour. *Serves 6*

Salmorejo

700g (1lb 9oz) ripe vine-ripened tomatoes, cored, tops nicked in a cross shape
3 cloves garlic, pounded to a paste
1 handful fresh breadcrumbs, made with French bread torn into small pieces and whizzed in the food processor
4 tablespoons extra virgin olive oil
1 tablespoon sherry vinegar

Drop the tomatoes into boiling water for 20 seconds, drain them, cool with plenty of cold running water, slip the skins off, and discard the seeds.

Put all the ingredients into the food processor and process until smooth. Taste and season with salt and freshly ground black pepper. Reserve.

Tuna

juice of 1 lemon
1 teaspoon flaky sea salt
freshly ground black pepper
6 x 200g (7oz) slices fresh tuna
olive oil for frying
plain flour for dusting

Rub the lemon juice, salt and pepper over the fish and set aside for 20 minutes.

Dust the fish with flour and panfry until well browned but medium rare. Drain on paper towels.

White Beans and Mint

400g (14oz) white haricot beans, soaked in cold water overnight
1/2 each carrot, stick celery and peeled onion
1 bay leaf
1 small handful parsley stalks
500ml (18fl oz) well-flavoured liquid chicken stock
1 small handful mint, chopped when needed
2 cloves garlic, very finely chopped
flaky sea salt and freshly ground black pepper
50ml (2fl oz) extra virgin olive oil

Drain the beans well, then put them in a pan with plenty of water along with the carrot, celery, onion, bay leaf and parsley stalks and boil until tender. Drain, discard the carrot, celery, onion, bay leaf and parsley stalks, and add the chicken stock.

Put onto the heat and boil, stirring continually, until the chicken stock has almost evaporated but the beans are still very moist. Remove from the heat, and stir in the mint, garlic, salt, pepper and olive oil.

Serve the tuna slices cut in half, sitting on the beans, with the sauce on the side.

or use thin slices of white veal instead of tuna
or use the Salmorejo as a soup to serve 4 – chill it and serve with a garnish of thinly sliced roasted red capsicums, chopped hard-boiled eggs and paper-thin slices of Serrano ham (like prosciutto), or to make a heartier dish, cold slices of boiled waxy potatoes or thinly sliced cold poached chicken breasts, drizzled with extra virgin olive oil.

Monkfish on Steamed Potatoes with Green Salsa

Hardly a recipe but a delicious mix of three simple layers – fluffy, floury steamed potatoes, barbecued or panfried monkfish with its prawn-like texture, and a topping of a tart, crunchy green salsa. Salmon fillets or most firm white fish are suitable for this dish, though the texture of monkfish makes it particularly good.

Serves 6

Salsa

½ cucumber, seeded, peeled and
*   finely diced*
3 tablespoon capers, drained
finely grated zest and juice of
*   1 large lemon*
2 spring onions, thinly sliced
4 tablespoons each of finely chopped
*   flat-leafed parsley and mint*
125ml (4fl oz) extra virgin olive oil
flaky sea salt and freshly ground
*   black pepper*

Mix all the ingredients together well, seasoning with the salt and pepper.

Monkfish and Potatoes

900g floury potatoes, peeled and cut into
*   bite-sized pieces*
6 x 150g (5oz) pieces very fresh skinned,
*   boned monkfish fillets*
4 tablespoons olive oil
finely grated zest of 1 lemon
½ teaspoon finely chopped rosemary tips

Put the potatoes on a plate in a large bamboo steamer over a high heat and steam until tender so that they are ready when the fish is cooked.

Toss the fish, olive oil, lemon zest and rosemary together and barbecue or panfry over a moderate heat until the fish is just cooked through. Do not overcook it and remember it will continue to cook a little after it is removed from the heat.

To serve, put the hot potatoes onto a warm platter, put the fish down the middle and drizzle the salsa over everything.

or *use the salsa on a 600g (1lb 5oz) piece of fillet steak which has been rubbed with garlic and pepper, barbecued in one piece until medium rare, rested, thinly sliced and served on salad greens and sliced tomatoes*

or *poach a chicken in salted water with a carrot, an onion, a stick of celery, peppercorns and a fresh bay leaf, then serve the carved, cooked chicken topped with the salsa and with rice on the side.*

Monkfish with Spicy Salt

This recipe was inspired by a lip-smacking dish on the menu at a restaurant in Hong Kong. Firm white fish (the prawny texture of monkfish is perfect, but any fish that won't fall to pieces when cooked will do) is marinated in a sweet and sour tamarind mixture then fried and served with a salty mix of chillies and peanuts. *Serves 6*

Spicy Salt

3 tablespoons peanut oil

2 large fresh mild red chillies, finely sliced

1 small fresh red chilli, finely sliced

1/2 green capsicum (pepper), cored, seeded and cut into 1/2cm (1/4in) dice

4 cloves garlic, finely chopped

75g (3 oz) chopped, roasted, unsalted peanuts

1/4 teaspoon Chinese five spice powder

2 tablespoons flaky sea salt (not rock salt)

1/2 teaspoon Szechuan peppercorns, toasted and coarsely ground

Heat the peanut oil in a large frying pan until hot. Add the chillies, capsicum, garlic, peanuts and five spice powder, and stir over a moderate heat until everything is starting to brown. Add the salt and peppercorns, mix well, and remove from the heat.

Fish

3 tablespoons flaky sea salt

2 carrots, shaved into paper thin ribbons

1 1/2 cucumbers, peeled, seeded and sliced paper thin

4 tablespoons tamarind concentrate

1 tablespoon sugar

1 tablespoon finely chopped ginger

2 cloves garlic, finely chopped

700g (1lb 9oz) boned monkfish, skin on, cut into 10cm (4in) long pieces

plain flour for dusting

4 tablespoons peanut oil

lime halves for squeezing

Sprinkle the salt over the carrot and cucumber, mix well and set aside for 20 minutes. Rinse well under cold water and squeeze dry, then put them in a serving dish.

Mix the tamarind, sugar, ginger and garlic and coat the fish with this. Set aside for 10 minutes, then dust with flour.

Heat the peanut oil in a large frying pan and fry the fish until browned on each side and cooked through. Remove from the pan and put the fish onto the carrot and cucumber.

Sprinkle the fish with some of the Spicy Salt and serve with lime wedges. Serve the remainder of the salt in a dish on the side.

or serve with steamed long grain white rice and a stirfry of baby bok choy which has been quartered lengthways, sliced spring onions, thinly sliced garlic, ginger and a splash of light soy sauce

or use the salt to flavour egg noodles which have been moistened with a little chicken broth

or use the marinade with panfried thinly sliced chicken breast or prawns and serve with the remaining salt on the side, a platter of raw thinly sliced carrots, cucumber, red capsicum, tomatoes and Cos lettuce leaves, and steamed rice.

Gurnard with Tomatoes, Basil and Broad Beans

Gurnard is sweet and delicious. Cooking the fish with the skin on keeps it moist and holds it together. This is a great dish for a quick mid-week family dinner, even though you have to peel the beans. For years I disliked broad beans until I tried them cooked and peeled. This way they are sweet and a beautiful colour, so although peeling them may be a labour of love it is worth it. Frozen broad beans are fine to use. *Serves 6*

250g (8 3/4 oz) broad beans
4 tablespoons extra virgin olive oil
6 large fillets of gurnard, skin on, bones
    pulled out with tweezers
plain flour
2 cloves garlic, thinly sliced
100ml (3 1/2 fl oz) dry white wine
6 large vine-ripened tomatoes, halved,
    cored, seeded and diced
100ml (3 1/2 fl oz) well-flavoured liquid
    chicken stock
flaky sea salt and freshly ground
    black pepper
1 tablespoon butter
handful basil leaves

Blanch the beans for 4 minutes in boiling water, drain, refresh in cold water and peel.

Heat the extra virgin olive oil in a frying pan over a moderate heat. Lightly dust the fish fillets with flour and panfry the fish until golden on both sides and just cooked. Remove from the pan and put the fish on a warm serving platter.

Add the garlic to the pan and fry until it just starts to brown. Add the wine, bring to the boil, and add the tomatoes and beans.

Add the stock, bring to the boil, simmer for 15 seconds, season with salt and pepper, stir in the butter and pour over the fish.

Sprinkle the basil leaves on top and serve immediately.

or serve with hot rice or couscous
or use panfried chicken breast instead of fish, but make sure the temperature of the pan is lower as the chicken will take much longer to cook
or in a little white wine steam open 12 live mussels, scrubbed, beards pulled out. Remove from the shells, pull out the brown tongues and thinly slice the mussels. Strain and reserve 100ml (3 1/2 fl oz) of the mussel cooking liquid. Make the recipe but add the mussel liquid instead of the wine, add the sliced mussels with the stock and proceed.

South-East Asian Sweet and Sour Baked Whole Snapper

The fish is stuffed with aromatic South-East Asian herbs, foil-wrapped and baked, then served with a chunky, hot sweet and sour dressing.

Buying a whole fish is more economical than buying fillets. It is easy to serve and eat – just start on one side, then turn it over for the other side. Be careful of the bones, and have some dry bread on hand for anyone to eat if they think they have swallowed a bone. *Serves 6*

Fish

4 slices fresh ginger

2 bulbs lemongrass, crushed

4 kaffir lime leaves

2.5 kg (5lb 8oz) gutted and scaled whole snapper, slashed to the bone 3 or 4 times on each side, head cut off if you prefer

4 tablespoons fish sauce

Preheat the oven to 220°C (425°F).

Put the ginger, lemongrass and lime leaves inside the fish and place it on a large oiled piece of tin foil in a roasting dish. Sprinkle with the fish sauce. Wrap so that it is sealed.

Bake for 25 minutes or until the fish is just cooked through. Remove from the oven and carefully slide the fish onto a warm platter.

Dressing

150ml (5fl oz) fresh lime juice

75g (3oz) finely grated palm sugar

1/2 teaspoon flaky sea salt

2 red onions, finely chopped

1/2 cucumber, seeded, peeled, cut into 1cm (1/2 in) dice

2 cloves garlic, finely chopped

1 handful cherry tomatoes, halved

small handful coriander leaves, chopped

1 teaspoon chopped Vietnamese mint

1 small fresh red chilli, thinly sliced

Mix the lime juice, palm sugar and salt together until all is dissolved. Add the remaining ingredients and mix well.

Garnish

75g (3oz) roasted unsalted peanuts, chopped

Pour the dressing over the hot fish, sprinkle with the peanuts and serve.

or serve with plenty of hot steamed white jasmine rice

or the dressing can be used on all sorts of grilled or barbecued food, and is good with thinly sliced steak or chicken

or omit the fish but cook 400g (14oz) jasmine rice and toss it with 24 shelled prawns which have been poached in a little salted water. Put the rice and prawns on a warm platter, make double the dressing and spoon it over the rice, top with plenty of the peanuts and serve the warm rice and prawn salad immediately to 6–8 guests as a first course.

Chicken with Red Vegetables and Prunes

I like the sweet and sour flavours and the deep red colour of this easy dish of browned chicken pieces baked on vegetables. *Serves 6*

1.5kg (3lb 3oz) chicken, jointed
   (see page 154)
3 tablespoons olive oil
1 large red onion, thinly sliced
3 cloves garlic, finely chopped
125ml (4fl oz) red wine
200ml (7fl oz) balsamic vinegar
2 tablespoons brown sugar
1 teaspoon flaky sea salt
1 teaspoon cracked black pepper
1 small cinnamon stick
200g (7oz) pitted prunes
1/2 red cabbage, thinly sliced
1 large beetroot, peeled and cut into 2cm
   (1in) dice
1 carrot, peeled and cut into 2cm (1in) dice
250ml (9fl oz) well-flavoured
   chicken stock
chopped parsley for garnish

Preheat the oven to 200°C (400°F). Sauté the chicken pieces in a little hot olive oil until each piece is well browned, then set aside.

Heat the olive oil in a wide saucepan, add the onion and garlic and sauté until the onion is soft. Add the wine, balsamic vinegar, sugar, salt, pepper, cinnamon and prunes and bring to the boil. Add the vegetables, mix well and simmer for 10 minutes.

Put the mixture into a casserole and put the chicken pieces on top. Pour the stock over. Cover and bake for 40 minutes.

Remove from the oven, sprinkle with parsley and serve with mashed floury potatoes, steamed long grain white rice or creamy polenta.

or *omit the chicken but add the stock to the saucepan, simmer the vegetables until tender and serve over panfried pork chops*

or *for a vegetarian option, do the same as above but add water instead of stock, add a 400g (14oz) can of rinsed, drained, red kidney or borlotti beans to the vegetables, and simmer until the vegetables are tender. Taste, season and serve with feta crumbled over the top and with the suggested accompaniments*

or *add some chopped rashers of rindless bacon or sliced carbonosi or frankfurter sausages with the onions, especially if you want to feed more people.*

Gratin of Chicken with Creamed Haricot Beans

This is a hearty dish of tarragon-flavoured chicken stew with a crisp breadcrumbed top, served with creamy white beans. *Serves 6*

Gratin

4 eggs
2 tablespoons olive oil
2 small leeks, thinly sliced
1 small carrot, cut into 1cm (1/2 in) dice
3 cloves garlic, finely chopped
zest of 1 lemon, finely chopped
1 tablespoon dried tarragon
1 tablespoon chopped flat-leafed parsley,
  plus extra for garnishing
5 single skinless, boneless chicken breasts,
  cut into 3cm (1 1/4 in) dice
plain flour
125ml (4fl oz) white wine
200ml (7fl oz) well-flavoured liquid
  chicken stock
flaky sea salt and freshly ground
  black pepper
2 handfuls breadcrumbs
100ml (3 1/2 fl oz) melted butter

Preheat the oven to 200°C (400°F). Bring the eggs to the boil in cold water, boil for 7 minutes, cool in cold water and peel.

Heat the olive oil over a moderate heat in a deep frying pan. Add the leeks, carrot, two-thirds of the garlic, the lemon zest, tarragon and parsley. Sauté, without browning, until the leeks are soft.

Dust the chicken with flour, add to the pan, mix well, and sauté until the chicken has coloured all over. Stir in the wine and stock and season with salt and pepper. Bring to the boil and simmer for 5 minutes. Pour the chicken mixture into a flat baking dish about 20 x 28cm (8 x 11in).

Chop the eggs and mix into the crumbs with the remaining garlic and sprinkle all over the chicken. Drizzle the melted butter evenly over the top.

Bake until the top is well browned and the chicken mixture is bubbling. Remove from the oven and sprinkle with chopped parsley.

Beans

400g (14oz) haricot beans, soaked in cold
  water overnight
1 small carrot
1 small onion
1 stick celery
1 fresh bay leaf
100ml (3 1/2 fl oz) white wine
220ml (8 3/4 fl oz) cream
finely chopped zest of 1 lemon
flaky sea salt and freshly ground black
  pepper
3 tablespoons chives, chopped into 2cm
  (1in) lengths

Put the beans, carrot, onion, celery and bay leaf into a large saucepan. Cover with plenty of water, bring to the boil and simmer until the beans are well cooked but not disintegrating. Drain well and return the beans to the saucepan. Discard the vegetables and bay leaf.

Add the wine, cream and lemon zest and bring to the boil. Season well with salt and pepper and simmer, stirring until the cream thickens. Add the chives and mix well.

Serve the gratin with the beans beside it.

or *add 200g (7oz) sliced portobello mushrooms*
  to the chicken dish with the leeks
or *serve the beans with roast lamb instead of*
  the chicken
or *use 800g (28oz) flaked boneless smoked fish*
  instead of the chicken.

Arroz con Pollo

This is my version of a sensational dish I ate in Spain. With a light first course and a salad to follow, it makes a special dinner.

It is like a paella, which is a flavour base of slow-cooked vegetables, flavourings and in this case chicken, with Calasparra rice added and then everything simmered in stock.

Although chicken is an important ingredient, like risotto, this is a dish where the rice is the star because of its quality. That rice could be the most important part of the dish is a difficult concept for some people, but when you use Calasparra rice and cook the dish carefully, one taste will convince you. *Serves 6*

4 tablespoons olive oil

1 small carrot, cut into 1cm (1/2 in) dice

1 small leek, thinly sliced

1 onion, finely chopped

4 cloves garlic, finely chopped

2 tablespoons sweet Spanish smoked paprika

1/2 teaspoon saffron, toasted and powdered (see page 156)

1 teaspoon flaky sea salt

3 single chicken breasts (about 600g, 1lb 5oz), sliced across the grain into 1cm (1/2 in) thick slices

finely grated zest of 1 lemon

3 cups Calasparra rice, well washed and drained

2 tablespoons tomato paste

1 roasted red capsicum (pepper), peeled, cored, seeded and cut into 1cm (1/2 in) dice

1.25 litres (44fl oz) boiling well-flavoured liquid chicken stock

500ml (18fl oz) boiling water

Heat the olive oil in a paella dish or wide frying pan. Add the carrot, leek, onion and garlic and gently fry, without browning, until the onion is soft.

Add the paprika, saffron and salt and mix well. Add the chicken and lemon zest and continue cooking until the chicken is well coloured, but not brown.

Add the rice, tomato paste and capsicum and mix well. Add the boiling stock and water and bring to the boil, stirring.

Stop stirring and simmer for 15 minutes until the rice has cooked and the mixture is thick. Serve immediately.

or use 400g (14oz) finely diced skinned pork loin instead of chicken

or mix in leftovers with a little beaten egg and fry in hot oil like fritters

or instead of chicken use fish or seafood or a mixture of both – 400g (14oz) skinless, boneless firm white fish fillets, cut into 5cm (2in) pieces and 12 large shelled prawns. Panfry the fish and prawns in olive oil until they colour, remove from the pan and reserve. Five minutes before the rice is cooked, stir in the seafood, let it cook through, then serve. Chicken stock is fine to use with seafood.

Chicken Supremes with Moroccan Salad

A chicken supreme is the breast with the wing bone left in but the wing tip removed. It is tastier than a boneless breast, as chicken cooked on the bone always tastes better.

I love the tart and juicy salad, which is more like a chunky sauce. *Serves 6*

Chicken

3 tablespoons cumin seeds
finely grated zest and juice of 2 lemons
4 cloves garlic, finely chopped
2 small dried red chillies, thinly sliced
50ml (2fl oz) olive oil
1 teaspoon cracked black pepper
1 tablespoon ground turmeric
6 organic chicken supremes

Toast the cumin seeds in a dry pan until fragrant and slightly darkened in colour.

Put all the ingredients except the chicken into a bowl and mix well. Add the chicken and toss to cover with the marinade. Marinate overnight or for a minimum of 1 hour.

Barbecue the chicken over a moderate heat or panfry until cooked.

Salad

1/2 large cucumber, peeled, seeded and cut
  into 1cm (1/2 in) dice
4 vine-ripened tomatoes, cored, seeded
  and cut into 1cm (1/2 in) dice
1 handful each coriander and flat-leafed
  parsley, coarsely chopped
1 clove garlic, finely chopped
24 Greek green olives, each flattened
  enough to make the flesh split
2 tablespoons toasted sesame seeds
100ml (3 1/2 fl oz) extra virgin olive oil
4 tablespoons lemon juice or to taste
flaky sea salt and freshly ground
  black pepper

Mix all the ingredients together, seasoning well with the salt and pepper.

Serve the chicken with the salad spooned over the top.

or use the same marinade for skinless, boneless
    firm white fish fillets, such as monkfish,
    snapper or hapuku, and serve it with the salad
or serve the salad on barbecued steak or lamb
    shortloins or racks which have been rubbed
    all over with crushed garlic
or serve the chicken and salad over couscous
    or rice.

Chicken Breasts with Prosciutto and Marsala

Prosciutto, Marsala and rosemary are a great combination of flavours and go well on chicken. If prosciutto is unavailable, use ham or bacon. *Serves 6*

4 tablespoons olive oil

6 single organic chicken breasts (about
   200g, 7oz each), dusted with plain flour

flaky sea salt

3 red onions, finely chopped

3 cloves garlic, finely chopped

1 teaspoon finely chopped rosemary tips

1 carrot, peeled and finely diced

1 stick celery, thinly sliced

100g (3 1/2 oz) prosciutto, chopped

150ml (5fl oz) dry Marsala

250ml (9fl oz) well-flavoured liquid
   chicken stock

2 tablespoons butter

1 tablespoon chopped flat-leafed parsley

flaky sea salt and freshly ground
   black pepper

Preheat the oven to 200°C (400°F).

Heat 2 tablespoons of the olive oil in a frying pan over a moderate heat and add the chicken breasts. Panfry until well browned, remove and put into a small roasting dish, sprinkle with salt and place in the oven. Roast for 10 minutes or until cooked through.

Meanwhile put the pan back on the heat, add the remaining 2 tablespoons of olive oil and add the onion, garlic, rosemary, carrot, celery and prosciutto. Fry gently, without browning, until the onions are soft.

Add the Marsala and boil until it is almost all evaporated. Add the stock and gently boil until the mixture is thick and the carrot is tender. Stir in the butter and parsley, taste and season with salt and black pepper.

Serve the sauce over the chicken breasts.

or omit the chicken part of the recipe and use the rest of the recipe over barbecued or panfried salmon fillet

or omit the chicken and use the rest of the recipe over hot pasta, dusting with plenty of finely grated parmesan cheese

or thinly slice 900g (1lb 15 3/4oz) peeled floury potatoes. Olive oil a heavy casserole and pack the potatoes into it. Season well with salt and pepper and a crushed clove of garlic. Cover and bake for 1 hour at 200°C (400°F). Serve with the chicken breasts and a green salad on the side.

One-pot Chicken

This dish makes regular appearances on our dinner table and is liked by everyone – it's a great family recipe. I vary the vegetables depending on what's around. *Serves 6*

3 tablespoons olive oil
1.5 kg (3lb 5oz) chicken, jointed
(see page 154)
2 onions, chopped
2 cloves garlic, finely chopped
1 large sprig fresh thyme
1 fresh bay leaf
500ml (18fl oz) well-flavoured liquid
chicken stock
500ml (18fl oz) water
2 carrots, sliced 2cm (1in) thick
4 waxy potatoes, peeled and cut into 4cm
(2in) dice
150g (5oz) frozen peas
150g (5oz) frozen whole kernel corn
2 tablespoons cornflour dissolved in
4 tablespoons water
flaky sea salt and freshly ground
black pepper
2 tablespoons chopped parsley

Heat the olive oil over a moderate heat in a wide, deep saucepan and brown the chicken pieces all over. Remove them to a dish and set aside.

Add the onions, garlic, thyme and bay leaf to the pan and fry gently, without browning, until the onions are soft.

Add the stock, water, chicken pieces, carrots and potatoes and bring to the boil. Simmer for 20 minutes, then add the peas and corn. Bring back to the boil and simmer for 5 minutes.

Bring back to the boil and quickly stir in the cornflour mixture so that the liquid in the pan thickens slightly. Taste and season with salt and pepper. Stir in the parsley.

or *serve it with steamed rice and a good splash of Tabasco sauce*
or *make the dish go further by adding 3 or 4 sliced carbonossi or frankfurter sausages with the chicken*
or *turn the cooked dish into chicken pie by putting the mixture into a pie dish and covering the top with flaky pastry, brushing with beaten egg, making a couple of slits to let the steam escape and baking in a hot oven until well browned and puffed.*

Citrus Chicken with Ginger Vegetables

Every so often I teach a 'healthy cooking' class. The first thing I say at these times is that this is not the diet class (diets don't work) or the vegetarian class. The only concession I need to make to health when it comes to the sort of food I like is perhaps lowering the amount of oil I use. Good cooking using natural ingredients from scratch is generally healthy. Eating a wide variety of food, being moderate, classing some food as 'mental health food' (e.g. the occasional rich dessert) and not worrying too much generally leads to a healthy diet.

This chicken recipe is one from my healthy class. It is steamed chicken with lemony Asian flavours on vegetables which have been simmered with ginger and tossed in light soy sauce. *Serves 6*

Chicken
1 x 1.5kg (3lb 3oz) chicken, jointed
(see page 154)
3 cloves garlic, crushed
zest and juice of 1 lemon or 2 small limes
3 kaffir lime leaves, bruised

Mix all the ingredients together and set aside for 1 hour to marinate. Put the chicken pieces into a large Chinese steamer and steam over a high heat for 25 minutes or until well cooked.

Ginger Vegetables
3 golden kumara (sweet potatoes), peeled
and cut into 2cm (1in) dice
2 medium-sized carrots, cut into
2cm (1in) dice
2 tablespoons finely chopped ginger
2 handfuls spinach leaves
4 tablespoons light soy sauce

Put the kumara, carrots and ginger in a saucepan and just cover with water. Bring to the boil and simmer until most of the water has evaporated and the vegetables are tender.

Remove from the heat, add the spinach and soy sauce, and toss gently so the spinach wilts.

Garnish
75g (3oz) pumpkin seeds
¹/₄ teaspoon flaky sea salt
coriander leaves

Heat the pumpkin seeds in a dry pan over a moderate heat until they toast and pop, then cool. Put the pumpkin seeds and salt in a food processor and grind to a coarse powder. Reserve.

Serve the chicken on the vegetables, sprinkle the pumpkin seed powder on top and garnish with the coriander.

or serve the chicken on steamed jasmine rice with the pumpkin seed mixture and a big green salad on the side instead of the vegetables
or for a vegetarian option, add cubes of tofu to the vegetables with the spinach and omit the chicken
or use thick skinless, boneless firm white fish fillets instead of chicken.

Steamed Chicken and Vegetables in Lemon Soy Broth

This is based on one of my favourite Japanese recipes. *Serves 6*

10 skinless, boneless chicken thighs

150ml (5fl oz) sake

3 baby bok choy, each cut lengthways into
   6 equal pieces

1 handful snow peas

2 medium-sized carrots, sliced paper thin
   lengthways

300ml (10 1/2 fl oz) water reserved from the
   steamer after the chicken and vegetables
   have been steamed

300ml (10 1/2 fl oz) well-flavoured liquid
   chicken stock

4 tablespoons light Japanese soy sauce

4 tablespoons fresh lemon juice

2 spring onions, thinly sliced on the
   diagonal

finely grated zest of 1 lemon

Put the chicken in a bowl, add the sake and mix well. Marinate for 1 hour.

Set up a 30cm (11 1/2 in) bamboo steamer over briskly boiling water and spread the chicken thighs directly onto the bamboo grid in one layer. Steam the chicken, uncovered, for 8 minutes. Don't waste any of the sake used for marinating, spoon it over the chicken as it cooks.

Add the vegetables except the spring onions, cover and steam for a further 5 minutes or until the chicken is cooked. Remove the vegetables to a wide bowl, slice each chicken thigh into four and add to the bowl.

Working quickly, put the 300ml (10 1/2 fl oz) of the steaming water and the chicken stock into a saucepan and bring to the boil. Add the soy sauce and lemon juice, bring back to the boil and pour the broth over the chicken and vegetables.

Sprinkle spring onions and lemon zest on top.

or serve on hot noodles or with a bowl of rice
   served separately

or use fish, prawns, scallops or a mixture of
   seafood instead of chicken, but steam for a
   shorter time than chicken

or use spinach leaves, broccoli or cauliflower
   florets, bean sprouts, asparagus or thin sliced
   courgette instead of the specified vegetables
   in the recipe.

Tamarind Chicken Salad with Gingered Brown Rice

This is simply a chicken simmered with ginger, tossed in a sour tamarind and sesame dressing and served on soft gingery brown rice with raw vegetables. *Serves 6*

Rice

500g (1lb 2oz) brown rice, well washed
3 tablespoons peanut oil
1 onion, finely chopped
3 tablespoons finely chopped ginger
2 kaffir lime leaves
1 litre (1 pt15fl oz) well-flavoured liquid
   chicken stock

Soak the rice for 4 hours in plenty of cold water, then drain well.

Heat the peanut oil in a saucepan over a moderate heat and add the onion, ginger and lime leaves. Fry gently, without browning, until the onion is soft.

Add the rice and stock, bring to the boil, cover tightly, turn the heat down to the lowest setting and cook, without uncovering for any reason, for 40 minutes. Remove from the heat and let it stand, without uncovering, for 10 minutes. Uncover and fluff up with a fork.

Chicken

1.5 kg (3lb 3oz) chicken, washed inside
   and out, wing tips cut off
flaky sea salt
7cm (2 1/2 in) piece ginger, slightly squashed
3 litres (5pt) water

Sprinkle the chicken inside and out with salt. Set aside for 20 minutes.

Put the ginger and water into a saucepan and bring to the boil. Add the chicken and boil gently for 30 minutes. Remove from the saucepan, cover with a clean damp cloth, and leave until cool.

Remove the breast meat and pull apart into bite-sized pieces; cut the wings and legs into pieces.

Dressing

3 tablespoons tamarind pulp, cooled
3 tablespoons kecap manis
1 1/2 tablespoons sesame oil
1 clove garlic, finely chopped
1 small fresh green chilli, finely sliced

Mix all the ingredients together well. Reserve.

Salad

1 stick celery, very thinly sliced
1 red capsicum (pepper), cored, seeded,
   thinly sliced
1/2 cucumber, peeled, seeded and diced
1 carrot, cut lengthways into paper-thin
   ribbons
coriander sprigs
mint leaves

Put the chicken into a bowl and toss with the Tamarind Dressing.

Put the rice onto a warm platter with the celery, capsicum, cucumber and carrot on top. Pile the chicken on top and garnish with the herbs.

or *use the dressing for panfried or grilled chicken or fish served on noodles with a sprinkling of crushed roasted peanuts*

or *serve the dressing as a dipping sauce with the rice and salad, but serve with barbecued prawns instead of the chicken*

or *spread the dressing all over a chicken, place it in a deep casserole with 125ml (4fl oz) water, cover tightly, and bake at 200°C (400°F) for 1 1/2 hours or until the chicken is well cooked. Remove, break up the chicken and serve with rice and salad.*

Quail with Salsa alla Vallesana

On a trip to Venice I met the delightful Signora Fulvia Sesani di Sabato. The recipe for the salsa is one she very kindly gave me and is an example of the wonderful Venetian cooking that she teaches in her Palazzo Morosini. The salsa is a delectable illustration of the Venetian genius for dishes which are 'agrodolce' or sweet and sour. Don't be put off by the anchovies, they melt into a delicious, savoury background flavour.

This recipe is another example of several simple components put together to make a dish which seems more complicated than it is – it is simply the salsa, quails cooked in the oven on fried onion with wine and stock, boiled peas, gently fried thinly sliced pumpkin and grilled blanched radicchio. Not a traditional use of this very Venetian salsa, but one that works. *Serves 6*

Salsa

2 tablespoons extra virgin olive oil
1 small onion, finely chopped
15 anchovy fillets, rinsed well in cold water
1 sweet apple
50ml (2fl oz) water
75g (3oz) raisins, soaked for 2 hours in
  warm water, then squeezed dry
75g (3oz) toasted pine nuts
125g (4 1/2 oz) sugar
125ml (4fl oz) white wine vinegar
1 teaspoon dijon mustard

Quail

3 tablespoons extra virgin olive oil
3 cloves garlic, finely chopped
2 onions, finely chopped
6 quail, washed inside and out and dried,
  wing tips cut off
flaky sea salt and freshly ground black
  pepper
250ml (9fl oz) red wine
250ml (9fl oz) well-flavoured liquid
  beef stock

Heat the olive oil in a small heavy saucepan, add the onion and fry gently until soft. Add the anchovies and stir over a low heat until a paste is formed.

Peel, core and purée the apple in a blender or food processor with the water just before it is needed so it doesn't go brown. Add the raisins, pine nuts, apple, sugar and vinegar and bring to the boil. Simmer until reduced by half.

Remove from the heat and stir in the mustard. Set aside.

Makes about 2 cups

Preheat the oven to 180°C (350°F).

Heat the olive oil over a moderate heat in a metal casserole and add the garlic, onions and the quail, sprinkled with salt and freshly ground black pepper. Fry gently until the onions are soft and the quail are browned.

Add the wine and stock, bring to the boil and place in the oven for 45 minutes or until the quail are very tender and the liquid almost evaporated. Remove from the oven and keep warm.

Pumpkin

olive oil
12 x 1/2 cm (1/4 in) thick slices peeled
* pumpkin*

Heat the olive oil and fry the pumpkin until browned and tender. Drain well on paper towels.

Peas

300g (10 1/2oz) baby organic peas
olive oil
flaky sea salt and freshly ground
* black pepper*

Cook the peas in plenty of salted water. Drain well. Season with a little olive oil, salt and pepper.

Radicchio

3 radicchio, halved
finely chopped garlic
extra virgin olive oil for brushing
flaky sea salt and freshly ground
* black pepper*

Blanch the radicchio for 4 minutes in boiling water, then drain well. Mix a little garlic with some olive oil and brush the radicchio all over. Cook under a hot grill until well browned. Season with salt and black pepper.

Serve the quail with the vegetables around them and the sauce on the side.

or *serve with Italian rice (but not a risotto), boiled in chicken stock and tossed with a little butter, pepper and salt*
or *serve the sauce with panfried skinned, boned salmon fillets*
or *serve the sauce with roast duck or barbecued lamb racks and a crunchy salad of thinly sliced fennel, lettuce and parsley sprigs, dressed with a well-seasoned vinaigrette of lemon juice, extra virgin olive oil and a little crushed garlic.*

Roast Duck with Balsamic Gravy, Lentils and Bacon

This is a larger recipe, great for a big dinner on a special occasion. The duck is roasted in liquid which creates the stock for the gravy. The rich, tangy duck and the earthy flavour of the lentils and bacon are a very satisfying combination.

Puy lentils are the small dark green lentils from France. Brown or green lentils are also suitable. Don't use the bright orange-skinned split lentils, as they cook to a mush. *Serves 6–8*

Duck

2 x 1.5kg (3lb 5oz) ducks, head, neck,
    wing tips and feet cut off
1 large onion, 1 carrot, 1 stick celery, all
    unpeeled and coarsely chopped
4 cloves garlic, bruised
4 large sprigs thyme
250ml (3/4 fl oz) full-bodied red wine
1 1/2 cups (27fl oz) well-flavoured liquid
    beef stock
2 tablespoons cornflour dissolved in
    3 tablespoons water
balsamic vinegar to taste
flaky sea salt and freshly ground
    black pepper

Lentils and Bacon

400g (14oz) Puy lentils
4 1/2 onions
1/2 stick celery
1 small carrot
1 bay leaf
4 tablespoons olive oil
3 cloves garlic, finely chopped
finely grated zest of 1 lemon
4 rashers rindless bacon, diced
4 tablespoons chopped flat-leafed parsley
flaky sea salt and freshly ground
    black pepper

Cut a 'v' section in the tail area of each duck to completely remove the parson's nose and the oil glands. Rinse and dry the ducks inside and out.

Preheat the oven to 200°C (400°F). Put the vegetables, herbs, wine and stock into a deep roasting dish. Put the ducks on top, breast side down, and fill with water three-quarters of the way up the ducks. Roast for 1 hour, turn the ducks onto their backs and roast for 1 more hour. Remove the ducks and keep warm.

Strain the stock, discard the vegetables and herbs and let the stock cool and settle and the fat rise to the top so that you can remove it.

Bring the degreased stock to the boil in a wide pan and boil to reduce by about a quarter. Thicken slightly with a little of the cornflour mixed with water, bring to the boil and season well with balsamic vinegar, salt and pepper. Set aside.

Put the lentils, half an onion, the celery, carrot and bay leaf into a large saucepan and fill with plenty of water. Bring to the boil, simmer for 20 minutes, or until the lentils are tender. Remove from the heat, drain the lentils and discard the vegetables and bay leaf.

Heat the olive oil in a large frying pan over a moderate heat. Finely chop the remaining 4 onions and add them to the pan with the garlic, lemon zest and bacon. Gently fry the onions, without browning, until they are soft – this will take about 15 minutes.

Add the lentils and parsley, mix well, and reheat. Taste and season with salt and pepper.

Carve the duck and serve on the lentils with the sauce in a jug or bowl on the side.

or *omit the lentil dish and serve the ducks on plain steamed long grain white rice with a green salad for a lighter meal.*

Sour Poussins with Mozarabe Ratatouille

Here poussins are marinated in an eastern Mediterranean-style marinade and roasted, while the so-called ratatouille is a slow-fried medley of vegetables and is a fusion of flavours from the vegetable stews of southern Spain, France and Italy. I called it Mozarabe because I liked the name and its Spanish-Moorish associations. *Serves 6*

Poussins

4 tablespoons sumac
4 cloves garlic, crushed to a paste
250 ml (9fl oz) plain unsweetened yoghurt
1 teaspoon flaky sea salt
6 poussins, split in half lengthways,
*   backbone discarded, wing tips cut off*

Mix the sumac, garlic, yoghurt and salt and spread all over the poussins. Marinate overnight or for a minimum of 2 hours.

Preheat the oven to 220°C (425°F). Put the poussins in a wide roasting dish in one layer and roast for 35 minutes or until well cooked and browned.

Ratatouille

1 large eggplant (aubergine), cut into
*   2cm (1in) dice*
flaky sea salt
olive oil for frying
5 courgettes (zucchini), sliced
1 red and 1 yellow capsicum (pepper),
*   cored, seeded and sliced*
2 red onions, diced
3 cloves garlic, finely chopped
1 tablespoon toasted coriander seeds,
*   ground*
2 tablespoons finely chopped ginger
grated zest of 1 orange
1 teaspoon cracked black pepper
1 teaspoon sweet Spanish smoked paprika
4 tablespoons roasted pine nuts
3 tablespoons currants
2 sticks celery, sliced

400g (14oz) can Italian tomatoes in juice,
*   mashed*
4 tablespoons capers, drained
3 tablespoons sugar
125ml (4fl oz) sherry vinegar
1 small handful each mint and basil
*   leaves, plus extra for garnishing*

Sprinkle the aubergine with salt, mix well, and leave to drain for 30 minutes. Rinse well in cold water and dry well.

Fry the eggplant, courgettes and capsicums separately in a little olive oil until each is browned, drain well and remove to a bowl.

Clean the pan and put in another 4 tablespoons of olive oil and add the onions, garlic, coriander, ginger, orange zest, pepper, paprika, pine nuts and currants. Fry gently until the onions are soft.

Add the celery and fry for 2 minutes. Add the tomatoes, capers, sugar and vinegar and bring to the boil. Simmer for 5 minutes.

Add the eggplant, courgettes and capsicums and bring back to the boil. Simmer for 5 minutes. Stir in the mint and basil leaves.

Serve the poussins on the ratatouille on a big white platter with extra mint and basil leaves sprinkled on top for a special dinner.

or *serve with rice or couscous*
or *the poussins are great (without the ratatouille) for lunch with warm pita bread and a fresh green salad.*

Warm Lamb Shanks and Barley Salad with Rocket Dressing

This is a filling one-dish meal, but it is a salad because it has a dressing – deliciously tart, green and nutty. The meat part can be made well in advance and reheated in its cooking liquid. The barley can also be cooked in advance and reheated. *Serves 6*

Lamb

8 boned lamb shanks (see page 105)
4 tablespoons olive oil
juice of 1 lemon
3 cloves garlic, chopped
2 fresh bay leaves
125ml (4fl oz) water
flaky sea salt and freshly ground
*   black pepper*

Preheat the oven to 190°C (375°F).

Put all the ingredients into a roasting dish, mix well, cover tightly, and bake for 2 hours. Remove from the oven, cool slightly, and break up the lamb shanks into bite-sized pieces. Discard the flavourings and liquid from the pan.

Salad

400g (14oz) well-washed pearl barley
20 stuffed olives
4 tablespoons chopped flat-leafed parsley
1 handful cherry tomatoes, halved
1/2 cucumber, halved lengthways, seeded
*   and chopped*
3 spring onions, finely sliced
2 sticks celery, thinly sliced

Boil the barley for 45 minutes until tender, drain well, and keep warm. Mix the warm barley with the other ingredients.

Dressing

2 handfuls rocket leaves, chopped
2 cloves garlic, chopped
3 tablespoons extra virgin olive oil
250ml (9fl oz) plain unsweetened yoghurt
zest and juice of 1 lemon
75g (3oz) roasted pecans
flaky sea salt and freshly ground black
*   pepper to taste*

Put all the ingredients into a food processor and blend until smooth.

To serve, put the salad on a platter, pile the warm lamb shanks on top and drizzle with the dressing.

or use rice instead of barley
or use the lamb shanks as a meat dish with
*   vegetables.*

Lamb with White Wine, Onions, Mint and Roasted Pumpkin

This dish is dead easy – just a sweet and sour onion relish, roasted pumpkin and panfried lamb with its pan juices. The success of the dish relies on three simple components which go together well. *Serves 6*

Onions and Mint
3 tablespoons olive oil
6 red onions, thinly sliced
4 tablespoons vinegar
250ml (9fl oz) water
3 tablespoons brown sugar
flaky sea salt and freshly ground
*   black pepper*
1 small handful mint leaves, chopped

Heat the olive oil over a moderate heat, add the onions and sauté, without browning, until they have softened. Add the vinegar and water, bring to the boil, and simmer until the onions are very soft and the water has evaporated.

Add the sugar, mix well, and season with salt and pepper. Stir in the mint leaves just before serving. Remove from the heat.

Pumpkin
1 kg (2lb 3oz) peeled, seeded pumpkin, cut
*   into 4cm (1 3/4 in) dice*
olive oil
flaky sea salt and freshly ground
*   black pepper*

Preheat the oven to 200°C (400°F). Toss the pumpkin in olive oil and season with salt and pepper. Roast until tender and browned, shaking the pan occasionally – about 40 minutes.

Lamb
2 cloves garlic, finely chopped
1 teaspoon freshly ground black pepper
4 tablespoons olive oil
5 x 200g lamb shortloins, all fat and sinew
*   removed*
250ml (9fl oz) white wine
125ml (4 fl oz) well-flavoured liquid
*   beef stock*

Mix together the garlic, pepper and olive oil and rub all over the lamb. Set aside for 20 minutes.

Heat a large heavy frying pan until hot and brown the lamb all over. (You don't need oil in the pan as it is already on the lamb.) Reduce the heat a little and cook the lamb for about 5 minutes on each side until medium. Remove the lamb and let it rest for 10 minutes in a warm place.

Pour the fat from the pan and put the pan on a high heat. Add the wine and stock and bring to the boil, stirring the pan with a wooden spoon to dislodge any caramelised bits adhering to the pan. Boil until reduced and a slightly syrupy consistency. Slice the lamb thinly across the grain of the meat and serve it beside the pumpkin with the onion on top. Pour the sauce over. Garnish with mint sprigs.

or *serve with rice or couscous and a big green*
*   salad*
or *use lamb racks instead of shortloins*
or *use the onions and mint with any barbecued*
*   chicken, lamb or steak.*

Spiced Lamb Rack with Vegetable Sofrito and Lemon Jam

This simple combination of three small recipes – the Lemon Jam is ridiculously simple – produces a dish which is easy enough for an everyday meal and grand enough for a special dinner. *Serves 6*

Lemon Jam

1 onion, finely chopped
2 tablespoons extra virgin olive oil
4 cloves garlic, finely chopped
1 teaspoon ground turmeric
2 small red dried chillies, finely sliced
2 fresh bay leaves
2 lemons, very thinly sliced, pips removed
250g (8 3/4 oz) sugar
250ml (9fl oz) water
pinch of flaky sea salt

Put all the ingredients into a saucepan and bring to the boil. Simmer for about 20 minutes until the mixture is thick and the water has evaporated. Remove from the heat, cool and reserve.

Sofrito

4 tablespoons extra virgin olive oil
1 onion, chopped
3 cloves garlic, finely chopped
1 cinnamon stick
1 carrot, finely diced
300g (10 1/2 oz) peeled, seeded pumpkin, cut into 2cm (1in) dice
3 medium-sized waxy potatoes, peeled and cut into 2cm (1in) dice
250ml (9fl oz) dry white wine
1 large handful spinach leaves
flaky sea salt and freshly ground black pepper

Heat the olive oil over a moderate heat and add the onion, garlic, cinnamon stick and carrot. Fry gently until the onion is soft.

Add the pumpkin, potatoes and wine. Cover and gently cook, stirring occasionally, until the potatoes and pumpkin are tender. Uncover and stir in the spinach leaves, cook until they wilt, taste and season with salt and pepper.

Lamb

2 teaspoons ground turmeric
3 tablespoons ground cumin
1 tablespoon ground ginger
1 teaspoon ground cinnamon
5 tablespoons extra virgin olive oil
6 x 6-bone frenched lamb racks, all fat and sinew removed
250ml (9fl oz) well-flavoured liquid beef stock
mint sprigs

Preheat the oven to 200°C (400°F). Mix the ground spices to a paste with the olive oil and rub all over the lamb racks.

Heat a frying pan over a high heat, add the lamb and sear it all over. Transfer it to a roasting dish and place in the oven for 10 minutes until medium done. Remove from the oven and let it rest in a warm place for 10 minutes.

Put the frying pan back over a high heat, add the stock and bring to the boil. Boil until slightly syrupy. Remove from the heat. Then carve each lamb rack into 3 double cutlets. Serve the lamb cutlets on the sofrito, with the meat sauce poured over and mint sprigs on top. Serve the Lemon Jam on the side.

or use the Lemon Jam like a spicy chutney with Indian food
or serve the sofrito with roast lamb, roast or panfried chicken or spicy sausages – also good with crumbled feta inside hot pita bread.

Lamb Shortloins with Greek Yoghurt and Sesame

Lamb shortloins are an easy cut of lamb to use as there is little waste and they cook quickly. Here they are marinated in yoghurt and spices.

The lamb can be barbecued on an oiled barbecue over a moderate heat if desired. *Serves 6*

Greek Yoghurt

300g (10 ½ oz) Greek yoghurt

1 clove garlic, crushed to a paste

flaky sea salt to taste

extra virgin olive oil for drizzling

3 tablespoons toasted sesame seeds,
    cooled

Mix the yoghurt, garlic and salt to taste. Put the yoghurt onto a shallow, wide plate and spread slightly. Drizzle well with extra virgin olive oil. Sprinkle the sesame seeds on top.

Set aside.

Lamb

6 lamb shortloins (about 200g, 7oz each),
    all fat and sinew removed

125ml (4fl oz) plain unsweetened yoghurt

2 tablespoons each toasted cumin and
    coriander seeds, ground coarsely

3 cloves garlic, crushed to a paste

3 tablespoons olive oil

6 large pieces fresh Indian or Middle
    Eastern flatbread

extra virgin olive oil

2 large handfuls rocket leaves

1 red onion, sliced

6 vine-ripened tomatoes, cored and cut
    into wedges

½ large cucumber, cut into chunks

1 small handful mint leaves

Put the lamb, yoghurt, ground cumin and coriander and garlic into a wide bowl and mix thoroughly. Marinate for a minimum of 30 minutes or maximum of overnight.

Heat the olive oil in a frying pan over a moderate heat and panfry the lamb until pink and juicy, about 4 minutes each side. Remove from the pan and let it rest for 10 minutes in a warm place.

Brush the flatbread with extra virgin olive oil and warm in a hot oven.

Put the rocket, onion, tomatoes and cucumber on a platter, leaving a space in the middle. Thinly slice the lamb and put it in the middle of the platter. Sprinkle the mint leaves on top of the lamb.

Serve with the Greek yoghurt and flatbread on the side. Eat the lamb and vegetables with a spoonful of yoghurt, wrapped in pieces of flatbread.

or instead of bread, serve a big bowl of steamed rice

or instead of lamb, use fish fillets fried until crisp and golden in olive oil or chicken breasts tossed in a little crushed garlic and sesame oil, barbecued and sliced

or use the Greek yoghurt as a dip with the warm flatbread as antipasto.

Lamb Shanks Braised with Pears and Silverbeet

Lamb shanks need long cooking but are such a succulent cut of meat that they never dry out. This is a staggeringly simple recipe where you throw everything into a casserole and the oven does the work.

To bone the shanks, slit the meat down one side of the bone, then cut the meat off it in one piece, or ask your butcher to do it.

In eastern Mediterranean cooking, fruits such as pears are cooked with meat and give it an appetising tartness. *Serves 6*

8 lamb shanks, boned

4 firm pears, peeled, cored and chopped into 3cm (1 1/4 in) pieces

zest of 1 large lemon

1 cinnamon stick

1 teaspoon ground turmeric

2 small dried red chillies, finely sliced

2 tablespoons finely chopped ginger

4 cloves garlic, chopped

1/2 teaspoon flaky sea salt

2 onions, chopped

750ml (27fl oz) well-flavoured liquid beef stock

1 tablespoon brown sugar

6 silverbeet (Swiss chard) leaves

Preheat the oven to 190°C (375°F).

Put all the ingredients except the silverbeet into a metal casserole and bring to the boil on the stove top. Cover well and place in the oven for 2 hours. Meanwhile, boil the silverbeet leaves until tender, cool in cold water, squeeze dry and chop.

Remove the casserole lid, stir in the silverbeet and cook for a further 30 minutes. Remove from the oven, let it stand for 5 minutes, then skim the fat off the surface.

or serve with couscous or rice and a salad to follow

or instead of the lamb use 1.5 kg (3lb 5oz) lean stewing beefsteak cut into 3cm (1 1/4 in) pieces

or add 400g (14oz) can rinsed, drained chickpeas to the mixture and cook as directed.

Lamb Shanks Baked with Garlic, Tomatoes and Chickpeas

This is my take on the one-pot stews for which the Spanish are famous. In this one the oven does all the work so that you end up with a delicious mix of tender lamb, creamy chickpeas and sweet nuggets of garlic, all in a fragrant, orangy tomato sauce. *Serves 6*

2 tablespoons extra virgin olive oil
10 cloves garlic, peeled
1 onion, chopped
1 carrot, chopped
2 teaspoons sweet Spanish smoked
  paprika
finely grated zest of 1 orange
8 lamb shanks, boned (see page 105)
250ml (9fl oz) well-flavoured liquid
  beef stock
125ml (4fl oz) red wine
400g (14oz) can Italian tomatoes, mashed
2 x 300g (10 1/2 oz) cans chickpeas, drained,
  washed and drained again
75g (3oz) currants
1/2 teaspoon flaky sea salt
1/2 teaspoon freshly ground black pepper

Preheat the oven to 200°C (400°F). Put all the ingredients into a deep casserole and mix well. Cover tightly and bake for 2 hours or until the lamb is falling apart. Remove from the oven, lift the lid and skim the fat from the top.

or *serve with crusty bread to mop up the juices, and a green salad*
or *use 400g (14oz) diced pork shoulder or loin, 6 chicken drumsticks and 4 chopped bacon rashers instead of the lamb, and serve with steamed rice*
or *serve with French couscous (see recipe on page 70).*

Chinese Braised Pork and Greens

I love those dishes of long-braised pork. Here is my untraditional interpretation with Chinese flavours. The pork is browned, mixed with the flavourings and liquid and cooked in the oven. This is an easy dish where the oven does the work. It can be made in advance as it reheats well. Just make it up to the point of adding the greens. When you want to serve it, bring it back to the boil and simmer for 5 minutes, then proceed with adding the greens. *Serves 6–8*

2 large Chinese dried mushrooms
200g (7oz) choy sum, thick ends cut off
1 small hot red chilli
5 cloves garlic
5cm (2in) piece ginger, chopped
1/2 teaspoon fennel seeds
1/2 cinnamon stick
1/4 teaspoon black peppercorns
1 star anise
2 tablespoons peanut oil
800g (1lb 12oz) lean skinned, boned pork
  shoulder, cut into 3cm (1 1/4 in) dice
2 tablespoons cornflour
4 tablespoons light soy sauce
4 tablespoons Shao Xing Chinese cooking
  wine or medium sherry
4 tablespoons brown sugar
375ml (13fl oz) well-flavoured liquid
  beef stock
250ml (9fl oz) water
5 spring onions, cut into 5cm (2in) lengths
100g (3 1/2 oz) snow peas

Soak the Chinese mushrooms in hot water until soft, discard the stalks, and thinly slice. Blanch the choy sum in boiling water for 3 minutes, refresh in cold water and drain well. Preheat the oven to 200°C (400°F).

Pound the chilli, garlic, ginger, fennel seeds, cinnamon, peppercorns and star anise until smooth (or if you do not have a mortar, finely chop the chillies, garlic and ginger and leave the spices whole).

Heat the peanut oil in a deep metal casserole and add the pork. Brown over a high heat, then add the pounded paste (or the finely chopped chillies, ginger, garlic and whole spices) and cornflour. Mix well and fry for 1 minute.

Add the soy sauce, Shao Xing wine, sugar, mushrooms, stock and water and bring to the boil. Cover and place in the oven for 1 1/2 hours or until the pork is very tender. If the mixture looks dry, add a little water. Remove from the oven, uncover, and skim off the fat.

Put onto the heat and bring to the boil. Add the spring onions, snow peas and choy sum and mix well. Simmer for 2 minutes until they are cooked but still crisp.

or *serve with hot jasmine rice*
or *leave the greens out of the recipe and serve with flatbread and a salad*
or *leave the greens out of the recipe and serve the dish with rice and Chinese greens (or any combination of vegetables that can be stirfried), which have been stirfried with garlic and a splash of oyster sauce.*

Twice-cooked Pork with Stalky Greens and Sticky Sesame Rice

The pork is cooked twice because it is first simmered with ginger to make it tender and fragrant, then marinated and stirfried with the stalky greens and served with sticky sesame rice. Plan for the rice and the greens to be ready at the same time. *Serves 6*

Pork

700g (1lb 9oz) skinned, boned belly pork
5cm (2in) piece ginger, squashed slightly
*   with the side of a chopper or large knife*

Put the pork and ginger into a saucepan and cover completely with plenty of water. Bring to the boil and simmer for 45 minutes until tender. Drain well, cool, and slice thinly across the grain.

Marinade

2 tablespoons peanut oil
1 teaspoon sugar
2 tablespoons finely chopped ginger
3 cloves garlic, finely chopped
5 tablespoons light soy sauce

Mix all the ingredients together well and pour over the pork slices, turning them over so that they are covered with marinade. Set aside for 30 minutes.

Rice

2 tablespoons sesame oil
3 cloves garlic, finely chopped
2 tablespoons finely chopped ginger
3 tablespoons black sesame seeds
100g (3 ½ oz) long grain white rice, well
*   washed and drained*
400g (14oz) glutinous white rice, well
*   washed and drained*
1 teaspoon flaky sea salt
625ml (22fl oz) water

Heat the sesame oil in a saucepan over a moderate heat. Add the garlic and ginger and stirfry for 20 seconds. Add the sesame seeds, the rices and salt and mix well. Add the water, mix well and bring to the boil.

Cover tightly, turn the heat to the lowest setting and cook, without uncovering, for 20 minutes exactly. Turn off the heat and let it rest, covered, for 5 minutes. Uncover and fluff up with a fork.

Greens

3 tablespoons Chinese salted black beans,
*   well washed under cold water and*
*   drained*
400g (14oz) choy sum or other stalky
*   Chinese greens, cut into 10cm (4in)*
*   lengths*
4 spring onions, ends trimmed, cut into
*   5cm (2in) lengths*

Heat a wok over a high heat and add the pork slices and the marinade. Stirfry until the liquid has evaporated and the pork has browned. Be careful not to burn the pork – if this starts to happen, lower the heat. Add the black beans, choy sum and spring onions. Stirfry until the vegetables are hot and wilted.

Serve the pork and rice with the vegetables and a small bowl of sweet Thai chilli sauce on the side.

or *the pork after its first cooking is good to eat just as it is – when cold it makes a great Vietnamese-style French bread sandwich filling with sweet chilli sauce and lettuce*

or *broccoli or cauliflower florets, thinly sliced courgettes or carrots, bean sprouts and button mushrooms are good alternative vegetables in the stirfried part of the pork recipe.*

Polpette con Verdura

Italians take all food seriously, and these meatballs or 'polpette' with vegetable sauce are no exception.

The polpette are browned in olive oil, then removed from the pan so that you can make the sauce of slow-fried vegetables, wine and stock. The polpette are then added to the sauce to finish cooking, then finally tender green vegetables are added. *Serves 6*

Polpette

250g (8 ³/₄ oz) lean beef topside
250g (8 ³/₄ oz) pork pieces
50g (2oz) breadcrumbs
100g (3 ¹/₂ oz) finely grated good quality
  parmesan cheese
2 eggs
3 cloves garlic, chopped
finely grated zest of 1 lemon
¹/₂ teaspoon flaky sea salt
1 small handful parsley leaves
100g (3 ¹/₂ oz) prosciutto, finely diced

Put all the ingredients, except the prosciutto, into a food processor and process until everything is finely minced. Mix in the prosciutto so that it is evenly distributed.

With oiled hands, roll the mixture into 4cm (1 ¹/₂ in) diameter balls. Dust the polpette with flour and set aside. *Makes about 24*

Sauce

500g (1lb 2oz) fresh or frozen broad beans
4 tablespoons olive oil
2 onions, finely chopped
1 carrot, finely diced
2 sticks celery, thinly sliced
zest of 1 lemon
1 clove garlic, finely sliced
2 fresh bay leaves
125ml (4fl oz) dry white wine
juice of 1 lemon
500ml (18fl oz) well-flavoured liquid
  chicken stock
1 large handful spinach leaves, sliced
3 tablespoons chopped Italian parsley
  flaky sea salt and freshly ground
    black pepper

Blanch the broad beans in boiling water for 2 minutes, drain, cool under running cold water and then shell.

Heat 3 tablespoons of the olive oil in a large frying pan over a moderate heat and brown the polpette. Remove them from the pan and add the remaining tablespoon of olive oil.

Add the onions, carrot, celery, lemon zest, garlic and bay leaves. Fry gently until the onions are soft.

Turn up the heat and add the polpette and wine. Let the wine bubble for 30 seconds, then add the lemon juice and stock. Simmer for 10 minutes until the sauce has thickened and the polpette and carrots are cooked.

Add the spinach and cook for 1 minute, then add the beans and the parsley. Simmer for 1 minute and season with salt and pepper.

or *make the meatballs from chicken, veal or pork or any combination of these meats*

or *use the sauce over chicken pieces that have been dusted with flour and panfried in olive oil with some chopped garlic and pepper*

or *serve the dish with buttered Italian rice which has been cooked by bringing 1 part rice to 2 parts water to the boil, turning down the heat to the lowest setting and cooking, covered, for 20 minutes, then uncovering, seasoning with salt and pepper and beating in a little butter.*

Risotto with Sausage, Vegetables and Prosciutto

In Italy risotto is usually a first course, but this one is so magnificent that I like serving it for a main course. However, this could be the first course of a special dinner.

Only genuine Italian short grained risotto rice (i.e. arborio or, even better, vialone nano or carnaroli) should be used to make risotto. *Serves 6*

4 tablespoons extra virgin olive oil
3 cloves garlic, finely chopped
1 tablespoon finely chopped rosemary tips
1 onion, finely chopped
1 small leek, thinly sliced
1 carrot, cut into 1cm (1 ½ in) dice
1 stick celery, thinly sliced
4 carbonossi sausages, sliced
*   2cm (1in) thick*
400g (14oz) arborio, vialone nano or
*   carnaroli rice*
150ml (5fl oz) dry white wine
1.5 litres (2pts 10 ½ fl oz) well-flavoured
*   liquid chicken stock, boiling*
2 handfuls rocket leaves
1 handful frozen peas, brought to the boil
*   and drained*
2 tablespoons unsalted butter
flaky sea salt and freshly ground
*   black pepper*
200g (7oz) very thinly sliced prosciutto
good quality parmesan cheese for grating

Heat the olive oil over a moderate heat and add the garlic, rosemary, onion, leek, carrot and celery. Fry gently until the onion is soft. Do not brown.

Add the carbonossi and rice and mix well for 2 minutes so that the rice 'toasts'.

Add the wine, turn the heat up and boil, stirring, until all the wine has evaporated.

Method 1 – for all types of Italian risotto rice
Start adding the boiling stock one ladleful at a time, stirring vigorously until the liquid has evaporated before adding the next ladleful. Continue until the rice is al dente and all the stock is used up – about 20 minutes.

Stir in the rocket, peas and butter, then taste and season.

Method 2 – for vialone nano and carnaroli rice only
Add all of the boiling stock and mix well. Turn the heat down to low, cover, and simmer for 15 minutes. Uncover and stir in the rocket, peas and butter, taste and season.

To serve, quickly pour the risotto onto a warm serving platter and spread the slices of prosciutto over the top to cover the risotto. Finely grate plenty of parmesan cheese on top and serve immediately.

or *use 2 diced, skinned, single chicken breasts instead of the sausages and omit the prosciutto*
or *omit the sausages and prosciutto and add the zest of a lemon and 250g (8 ¾ oz) sliced button mushrooms with the rosemary and proceed with the recipe*
or *omit the sausages, prosciutto and cheese and stir through 24 shelled prawns with the rocket, peas and butter, letting the prawns cook long enough to be cooked through.*

Baked Beans for Grown Ups

I had forgotten how easy it was to make the ultimate French comfort food, cassoulet, or rather to follow the method and use whatever was to hand, until I recently taught it at a cooking class. Here is my simplified version, which produces the most finger-lickin' succulent beans baked with garlic, tomato, pork, bacon, chicken and sausage. This is for those who enjoy the occasional flesh feast.

Because this is such a rich dish it goes a long way, needs only a green salad as accompaniment and reheats well. I don't soak the beans, but just cook them slowly. *Serves 6*

300g (10 1/2 oz) white haricot beans
3 onions, peeled
1 carrot
2 fresh bay leaves
8 rashers rindless bacon
4 tablespoons olive oil
4 cloves garlic
6 chicken drumsticks
400g (14oz) cubed, skinned, boned pork
    shoulder or loin
2 carbonossi sausages, sliced
125ml (4fl oz) dry white wine
3 tablespoons tomato paste
500ml (18fl oz) well-flavoured liquid
    beef stock
2 tablespoons chopped parsley
freshly ground black pepper
100g (3 1/2 oz) breadcrumbs

Put the beans, 1 onion, the carrot and the bay leaves into a large saucepan of water. Bring to the boil and simmer until the beans are tender but firm. This could take an hour, depending on the age and size of the beans. Drain well and discard the vegetables and bay leaves. Reserve the beans.

Preheat the oven to 190°C (375°F). Line the bottom and sides of a heavy casserole with the bacon. Set it aside.

Heat the olive oil over a moderate heat in a deep frying pan and chop the remaining 2 onions. Add the garlic and onions to the oil and fry gently, without browning, until the onions are soft. Add the chicken, pork and sausages, turn up the heat and brown everything.

Stir in the wine, let it bubble for a few minutes, then add the reserved beans, tomato paste, stock and parsley. Mix carefully but well. Add some black pepper and bring all back to the boil.

Put the mixture into the bacon-lined casserole and sprinkle the breadcrumbs evenly on top. Cover, place in the oven, and bake for 1 hour. Remove from the oven and serve.

or *make the dish with a jointed 1.5 kg (3lb 3oz) chicken (see page 154) instead of the bacon and the mixture of meat*
or *leave out the beans and serve with rice or potatoes for a lighter meal.*

Braciole alla Contadina

I served this to the family one year for Christmas dinner and everyone liked it. It is a big, rich dish but not hard to make, and it can be made in advance as it reheats well.

It is thin slices of veal rolled up with a stuffing, browned and cooked in a rich vegetable and tomato sauce. Prosciutto and provolone cheese are available in the supermarket. *Serves 6–8*

Stuffing

100g (3 1/2 oz) prosciutto, chopped
100g (3 1/2 oz) coarsely grated provolone
*   cheese*
4 cloves garlic, pounded to a paste
75g (3oz) sultanas
1 handful fresh white breadcrumbs
*   (whiz white bread in the food processor*
*   until it turns to crumbs)*
zest of 1 lemon
3 tablespoons chopped flat-leafed parsley
1/2 teaspoon cracked black pepper

Mix all the ingredients together well.

Veal Rolls

8 slices (about 600g, 1lb 5oz) veal schnitzel

Beat the schnitzel slices out a bit more with a meat mallet.

Put one-eighth of the stuffing at the end of each slice of veal, roll them up and tie securely with a piece of natural fibre string. Set aside.

Sauce

4 tablespoons extra virgin olive oil
2 cloves garlic, finely chopped
2 onions, finely chopped
2 small carrots, finely diced
2 courgettes (zucchini), finely diced
3 waxy potatoes, peeled and cut
*   into 2cm (1in) dice*
20 black olives
125ml (4fl oz) red wine
2 x 400g (14oz) cans Italian tomatoes in
*   juice, mashed*
250ml (9fl oz) well-flavoured liquid
*   beef stock*
250ml (9fl oz) water
flaky sea salt and freshly ground
*   black pepper*

Heat the olive oil over a moderate heat and brown the meat rolls. Remove them to a plate and add the garlic, onions, carrots, courgettes, potatoes and olives to the pan. Fry, without browning, until the onions are soft. Add the wine and bring to the boil. Boil for 1 minute and add the tomatoes, stock and water. Taste and season with salt and pepper.

Carefully pack the veal rolls into the sauce, bring to the boil, cover, turn the heat down and simmer for 2 hours.

Serve the veal rolls in sauce with crusty bread and a salad to follow.

or *you can eat the sauce over pasta as a first course and the veal rolls as the second course with a salad to follow.*

Fillet of Beef with Squash, Spinach and Soft Brown Rice

This marinated fillet steak has sweet and salty Japanese flavours. It is served with soft brown rice, which has had rather bad press as the food of self-punishing health freaks. If brown rice is soaked for 4–5 hours, it becomes fluffy and soft when cooked and its nutty flavour is easily appreciated.

Miso is a Japanese fermented soy bean paste and is available from Asian food shops. *Serves 6*

Rice
500g (1lb 2oz) short grain brown rice
1.25 litres (44fl oz) water

Soak the rice for 4–5 hours in plenty of cold water and drain well. Wash the rice well and drain again. Put the rice and measured water into a saucepan, bring to the boil, cover tightly, turn the heat down to the lowest setting and cook for 40 minutes. Do not uncover for any reason.

Remove from the heat and let it rest, keeping it covered, for 10 minutes. Uncover and fluff up with a fork.

Beef
3 tablespoons white miso
4 tablespoons mirin
1 tablespoon Japanese light soy sauce
600g (1lb 5oz) eye-fillet of beef in 1 piece, all fat and sinew removed
vegetable oil for frying

Mix the miso, mirin and soy sauce together and spread it all over the beef. Marinate for 1 hour.

Preheat the oven to 200°C (400°F).

Take the beef out of the marinade and brown all over in a hot pan in a little vegetable oil. Put into the oven in an oiled pan and roast, turning frequently, for 10–15 minutes, depending how rare you like it. Be careful it doesn't burn.

Remove from the oven and let it rest for 10 minutes in a warm place.

Squash and Spinach
500g (1lb 2oz) peeled, seeded, buttercup squash (or firm Orange Crown pumpkin), cut into 2cm (1in) pieces
4 tablespoons Japanese light soy sauce
4 tablespoons mirin
4 tablespoons water
1 teaspoon castor sugar
150g (5oz) spinach leaves

Boil the squash in water until almost cooked but still slightly hard in the middle, then drain well.

Put the soy, mirin, water and sugar into a wide pan. Add the squash and bring to the boil. Cover and simmer for 5 minutes, turning the squash pieces occasionally until they are tender.

Add the spinach leaves and cook, uncovered, until the spinach is well wilted. Remove from the heat.

Serve the thinly sliced beef on the rice with the squash and spinach around it.

or *replace the beef with chicken breasts which have been tossed in crushed garlic and soy oil, barbecued and sliced*
or *serve the squash and spinach with panfried salmon fillet*
or *stir some cubes of tofu through the squash and spinach at the last minute and serve on the rice for a vegetarian option*

Poached Beef and Vegetables with Harissa and Yoghurt

Here I've given a North African spin on the traditional French method of poaching beef in which I spice the poaching stock and use fiery harissa as the accompanying condiment. I like to lash out and use eye-fillet , but the other cuts of beef are good, too – just don't overcook them. *Serves 6*

Harissa

100g (3½ oz) small dried chillies, seeded
4 tablespoons each coriander and
  cumin seeds
6 cloves garlic
4 tablespoons flaky sea salt
extra virgin olive oil

Soak the chillies for 15 minutes in cold salted water, then drain well. Toast the coriander and cumin seeds separately in a dry frying pan until fragrant and slightly darkened, then grind coarsely. Put the chillies, spices, garlic and salt into a food processor and process, adding enough of the olive oil to make a creamy paste. Put into a small bowl and reserve.

Yoghurt

250ml (9fl oz) plain unsweetened yoghurt
4 tablespoons extra virgin olive oil
1 teaspoon sweet Spanish smoked paprika

Pile the yoghurt into a bowl, drizzle with the olive oil and sprinkle with the paprika. Reserve.

Beef and Vegetables

6 small tomatoes, cored, tops nicked in a
  cross shape
1 litre (1pt 15fl oz) well-flavoured beef stock
1 cinnamon stick
finely grated zest of 1 orange
3 cloves garlic, sliced
1 bay leaf
600g (1lb 5oz) piece eye-fillet, topside, scotch
  fillet or sirloin, fat and sinew removed
3 courgettes (zucchini), thinly sliced

12 button mushrooms
200g (7oz) green beans, stalk end trimmed
150g (5oz) frozen peas

Drop the tomatoes into boiling water for 20 seconds, drain, cool with plenty of cold running water and slip the skins off.

Put the stock, cinnamon, orange zest, garlic and bay leaf into a saucepan and bring to the boil. Add the beef and simmer for 10 minutes for medium rare. Remove the beef and let it rest in a warm place.

Bring the stock back to the boil and add the courgettes, mushrooms and beans, simmer for 2 minutes, add the peas and tomatoes and simmer for 2 minutes. Remove from the heat.

Strain the stock to remove the vegetables. Discard the cinnamon and bay leaf.

Put the vegetables on a warm deep platter. Slice the beef thinly and arrange on the vegetables. Moisten everything with the hot poaching stock but don't use it all as there will be too much. Freeze the remainder and use in a soup or stew. Serve the harissa and yoghurt on the side.

or *serve with steamed basmati rice or couscous*
  followed by a chunky salad of tomatoes,
  cucumber, thinly sliced carrots, sliced red
  capsicums, green olives and mint leaves with
  a dressing of extra virgin olive oil whisked with
  lemon juice, crushed garlic, salt and freshly
  ground black pepper
or *change the stock to chicken stock and the beef*
  to a cut-up chicken (it will take longer to cook),
  and serve with the same vegetables and
  accompaniments.

Barbecued Eye-fillet with Walnut and Anchovy Sauce

This is a deluxe barbecue dish designed around the Walnut and Anchovy Sauce. The steak is barbecued in one piece and then sliced, served with potatoes and fennel and accompanied by the tasty sauce. *Serves 6*

Sauce

16 anchovy fillets (Spanish are best)
75g (3oz) toasted walnut pieces
1 clove garlic
1 tablespoon sherry vinegar
1 handful each basil and flat-leafed parsley leaves
150ml (5fl oz) light olive oil or canola oil

In a blender or food processor, put the anchovies, walnuts, garlic, vinegar, basil and parsley. Process to a smooth paste. Add the oil slowly until it is all incorporated and the mixture is thick. Put into a small bowl.
Makes about 375ml (13fl oz)

Beef, Potatoes and Fennel

2 cloves garlic, crushed
1 tablespoon coarse cracked black pepper
4 tablespoons olive oil, plus extra for brushing
600g (1lb 5oz) eye-fillet of beef or other steak, in one piece, all fat and sinew trimmed off
800g (1lb 12oz) floury potatoes, peeled and sliced 2cm (1in) thick
2 bulbs fennel, trimmed and thinly sliced
1 red capsicum (pepper)
18 green olives
1 handful flat-leafed parsley sprigs

Rub the garlic, pepper and 4 tablespoons of the olive oil all over the beef and set it aside for 30 minutes.

Parboil the potatoes until almost tender, then drain well. Blanch the fennel in boiling water for 4 minutes, then drain well. Char the capsicum all round over a hot flame or under a grill, then peel, core, seed and slice.

Put the beef on a moderate barbecue and barbecue for 10–15 minutes, turning frequently. Remove and let it rest for 10 minutes in a warm place.

Meanwhile, brush the potatoes and fennel with olive oil and barbecue them both until the potatoes are tender and everything is well browned.

Place the potatoes and fennel on a warm platter. Slice the meat thinly and place on top of the vegetables. Sprinkle the capsicum, olives and parsley on top. Serve with the sauce on the side.

or *serve the sauce as a dip with raw vegetables and crusty bread*
or *serve the sauce with roast lamb and the white beans from the Tuna with Salmorejo and White Beans and Mint on page 72*
or *use boneless chicken breast instead of steak.*

Polenta with Meat Sauce

A rich dish for serious meat-lovers. The sauce is fine made the day before and gently but thoroughly reheated – its richness is a perfect complement to the yellow polenta. *Serves 6*

Meat Sauce

4 tablespoons olive oil
1 onion, finely chopped
1 carrot, cut into 1cm (1/2in) dice
2 sticks celery, cut into 1cm (1/2in) dice
2 cloves garlic, finely chopped
50g (2oz) prosciutto (or bacon), chopped
200g (7oz) chicken livers, cleaned of fat and sinew
400g (14oz) lean minced beef
125ml (4fl oz) full-bodied red wine
375ml (13fl oz) well-flavoured liquid beef stock
2 tablespoons tomato paste
flaky sea salt and freshly ground black pepper

Heat the olive oil in a frying pan over a moderate heat and add the onion, carrot, celery, garlic and prosciutto. Fry gently, without browning, until the onion is soft.

Turn up the heat and add the chicken livers and the minced beef. Fry until the livers are browned and the beef is crumbly. Break up lumps of mince with a wooden spoon but be careful not to mash the livers.

Stir in the wine and let it bubble for a minute. Add the stock and tomato paste and mix well. Bring to the boil and simmer for 15 minutes until the vegetables are soft and the sauce is thick. Taste and season with salt and pepper.

Polenta

1 litre water
1/2 teaspoon flaky sea salt
2 fresh bay leaves
200g (7oz) Italian yellow polenta

Bring the water, salt and bay leaves to the boil. Add the polenta in a thin stream, stirring continuously. Turn the heat down to a simmer and cook, stirring, for 20 minutes. Discard the bay leaves.

Serve the polenta spooned into bowls with the sauce on top.

or *serve the sauce on short tubular pasta cooked al dente instead of the polenta*

or *instead of water use milk in the polenta, add a handful of finely grated parmesan cheese and a finely chopped clove of garlic as it cooks, and serve with your favourite tomato pasta sauce and more parmesan cheese*

or *once the polenta is cooked, pour it out onto a wooden board and let it cool as a flat cake, then slice with a wet knife into 2cm (1in) thick slices, brush with olive oil and barbecue, grill or fry, and serve it instead of potatoes the next time you have a stew or braised meat dish that has a sauce.*

sweet plates

For me, recipes for sweet things should be classified as 'mental health' food – good for your spirit and designed to delight. They can mark the end of a special meal, they can stand alone as a celebration dish or they can be an indulgent snack between meals.

Prune and Mascarpone Tart with Orange Marmelatta

Marmelatta is Italian for marmalade, but the Italian version is not as bitter as the English one. Here it is perfumed with cardamom and cinnamon and reflects the Arab influence on southern Italian food. It goes well with the tart. Begin the Marmelatta a day in advance. *Serves 6*

Marmelatta

*2 oranges, cut into quarters, then each
    quarter thinly sliced*
4 cardamom pods, bruised
1 cinnamon stick
750ml (1pt 5fl oz) water
500g (1lb 2oz) sugar

Put the oranges into a large bowl and cover with cold water. Leave overnight, then drain well.

Put the oranges into a saucepan with the spices and the 750ml (1pt 5fl oz) water. Boil until the oranges are transparent and the water has evaporated by half, about 20 minutes.

Add the sugar and boil until the temperature is 104°C (220°F) or a spoonful of the mixture jellies on a cold plate, about 15 minutes. Remove from the heat, discard the spices and cool.
Makes about 500ml (18fl oz)

Pastry

4 tablespoons castor sugar
125g (4 1/2 oz) unsalted butter
finely chopped zest of 1 orange
1 egg
200g (7oz) plain flour

Put the sugar, butter and orange zest into a food processor and process until well creamed. Add the egg and process until smooth. Add the flour and process until it forms a ball. Remove and wrap the pastry in waxed paper. Refrigerate until firm.

Roll the pastry out on a well-floured surface and use it to line a 28cm fluted detachable-based flan ring. Refrigerate or freeze until the pastry is hard.

Bake blind at 180°C (350°F). If the pastry didn't get this precooking, it would never cook and be crisp because the filling is so wet. Remove from the oven and fill with the following.

Filling

400g (14oz) mascarpone
2 eggs, beaten
finely grated zest of 1 orange
100g (3 1/2 oz) castor sugar
300g (10 1/2 oz) pitted prunes

Beat all the ingredients, except the prunes, together until smooth. Mix in the prunes and pour into the pastry shell. Place into the oven and bake for 1 hour until set and well browned.

Remove from the oven and let the tart cool completely.

Serve a wedge of tart with whipped cream and a spoonful of Marmelatta.

or use halved dried figs instead of prunes in the filling and mix a teaspoon of fresh thyme leaves into the mascarpone mixture – the thyme goes well with the figs and orange
or use walnut halves instead of prunes
or serve the Marmelatta as they do in the eastern Mediterranean, as a dessert on small plates with a dollop of thick Greek yoghurt – it can be made with the equivalent amount of lemons, pink grapefruit, limes, kumquats or a mixture of any of these, and will keep like jam and makes a great gift.

Prune and Almond Tart

Although this tart looks and tastes as if you bought it from a French bakery, it is easy to make with no time-consuming baking blind required. The pastry is made, rested, rolled out, put into a tin, refrigerated until hard, filled with a mix of ground almonds, poached prunes, eggs and sugar, then baked. It is great warm as a dessert or at room temperature with a strong cup of coffee. *Serves 6–8*

Pastry
4 tablespoons castor sugar
125g (4 1/2 oz) unsalted butter
finely chopped zest of 1 lemon
1 egg
200g (7oz) plain flour

Put the sugar, butter and lemon zest into a food processor and process until well creamed. Add the egg and process until smooth. Add the flour and process just until it forms a ball. Do not over-process.

Remove from the processor and wrap the pastry in waxed paper. Refrigerate until firm.

Roll the pastry out on a well-floured surface and line a 28cm (11in) diameter fluted detachable-based flan ring with an even layer of pastry. Put the lined flan tin into the fridge or freezer until the pastry is hard.

Filling
300g (10 1/2 oz) pitted prunes
125ml (4fl oz) water
125ml (4fl oz) white wine
200g (7oz) unsalted butter
250g (8 3/4 oz) castor sugar
4 organic eggs, beaten
3 tablespoons plain flour
*300g (10 1/2 oz) almonds, ground finely in
    the food processor*
4 tablespoons dark rum

Preheat the oven to 150°C (300°F).

Put the prunes into a small saucepan with the water and wine and bring to the boil. Simmer for 4 minutes, remove from the heat and drain well. Discard the liquid and allow the prunes to cool completely.

Cream the butter and sugar, add the eggs and flour and beat well to incorporate. Stir in the almonds and cooled prunes.

Pour the mixture into the cold pastry shell and bake for 45 minutes or until the filling is set, well browned and slightly puffed up. Remove from the oven, sprinkle with the rum and cool.

Serve the tart in wedges with whipped cream.

or *this is delicious with 300g (10 1/2 oz) best-quality dark chocolate melted and drizzled over the top and allowed to harden before eating*

or *replace the prunes with 250g (8 3/4 oz) fresh raspberries*

or *replace the ground almonds with 300g (10 1/2 oz) long strand desiccated coconut for a coconut version of the tart.*

Warm Spiced Prune Devil's Food Cake with Baked Tamarillos

This is another devastatingly simple cake to make. It is devil's food cake that is so dark it is almost black, but it is not a strongly flavoured chocolate cake. It is, however, delicious and can be whipped up at a moment's notice. *Serves 6–8*

Cake

100g (3 1/2 oz) halved pitted prunes
190ml (7fl oz) boiling water
oil for the cake tin
1 teaspoon freshly ground cardamom
   seeds
1/2 teaspoon ground cinnamon
190g (6 3/4 oz) plain flour
400g (14oz) brown sugar
1/2 teaspoon flaky sea salt
2 teaspoons baking soda
50g (2oz) best-quality cocoa
250ml (9fl oz) yoghurt
4 tablespoons extra virgin olive oil
2 eggs, beaten
1 teaspoon pure vanilla extract

Soak the prunes in the boiling water for 20 minutes. Preheat the oven to 180°C (350°F). Oil and paper a 24cm (9 1/2 in) diameter springform cake tin.

Put the dry ingredients into a bowl and mix well, making sure there are no lumps of sugar.

Drain the prunes and add the liquid to the dry ingredients. Reserve the prunes.

Add the remaining ingredients, except the prunes, and mix well. Stir in the prunes. Pour into the tin and bake for 45 minutes or until a skewer comes out clean when inserted into the middle of the cake.

Remove from the oven and remove from the tin when cool enough.

Tamarillos

8 tamarillos with stems, skin nicked
150g (5oz) demerara sugar
juice of 1 orange

Bring a saucepan of water to the boil and add the tamarillos. Bring back to the boil and drain. Cover the tamarillos with cold water and, when cool enough, drain and peel them. Cut each tamarillo into quarters up to the stem but not right through.

Lie the tamarillos in a wide roasting dish. Sprinkle the sugar and juice on top and bake at 180°C (350°F) with the cake for 15 minutes or until syrupy. Remove from the oven.

Serve the warm cake in wedges with the tamarillos on the side and some Greek yoghurt.

or *use stoned fresh dates instead of prunes in the cake*
or *serve the cake with mascarpone and fresh raspberries*
or *serve the cake with Olive Oil Chocolate Mousse on page 151.*

Millefoglie Cinque Lune

In a small street just behind the Piazza Navona in Rome there is a bakery called the Cinque Lune (Five Moons) where I gorged myself on their delectable cakes. You have probably guessed that I have a fatal sweet tooth. Their cannoli – fried pastry tubes filled with ricotta, chocolate and dried fruit – were like a religious experience. Millefoglie, or mille-feuille as the French call them, are a specialty of Rome and I have called this one after the Cinque Lune because, like their pastries, this one is also delicious. *Serves 6*

Pastry
400g good-quality bought flaky puff
*   pastry, rolled into 2 x 25cm (10in)*
*   squares*
1 egg white
2 tablespoons castor sugar
4 tablespoons sliced almonds

Preheat the oven to 200°C (400°F). Put the pastry squares onto baking trays.

Lightly whisk the egg white and sugar together and paint it over one of the pastry squares. Sprinkle the almonds on top. Place both squares into the fridge until very cold.

Place the pastry into the oven and cook it as much as possible without burning it. Remove from the oven and cool.

Filling
3 egg yolks
100g (3 1/2 oz) castor sugar
4 tablespoons grappa or brandy
150g (5oz) roasted blanched almonds,
*   finely ground*
300ml (10 1/2 fl oz) cream, stiffly whipped

Beat the egg yolks and sugar until white in a large stainless steel bowl, adding the grappa a spoonful at a time, beating as you do it, until it is incorporated.

Put the stainless steel bowl over a low heat or a bowl of simmering water and stir until the mixture is thick and just catching on the bottom. Remove from the heat and stir in the almonds. Set aside to cool completely.

Fold the almond mix into the whipped cream and return to the fridge until it thickens up again.

Ricotta Mixture
200g (7oz) ricotta
finely grated zest of 1 orange
3 tablespoons castor sugar
75g (3oz) best-quality dark chocolate,
*   finely chopped*

Beat the ricotta, orange zest and sugar until smooth. Stir in the chocolate. Put into the fridge until it thickens again.

Assemble the millefoglie just before you want to eat it. Carefully trim the edges of the pastry with a sharp knife so that the two squares are the same size. Spread the ricotta mixture over the pastry square that doesn't have the almonds on top. Spread the almond cream on top of the ricotta. Put the almond-topped pastry square on top. Dust with icing sugar and serve.

or *if you're in a hurry and need a good-looking*
*   dessert fast, simply fill the pastry with a layer*
*   of blackcurrant jam, fresh blackberries or*
*   other berries and a layer of whipped cream*
or *use the almond cream as a luxurious topping*
*   for peeled sliced fresh white peaches*
or *add a layer of sliced strawberries to the*
*   fillings in the millefoglie.*

Rhubarb and Ricotta Cake

This can be made well in advance and is like a firm trifle in the shape of a cake which can be cut into wedges.
Serves 6–8

*500g (1lb 2oz) rhubarb, cut into 5cm
    lengths*
150g (5oz) castor sugar
200ml (7fl oz) white wine
*250g (8 3/4 oz) packet sponge fingers or
    savoiardi biscuits*
600g (1lb 5oz) ricotta, beaten smooth
12 amaretti biscuits, crumbled coarsely
*200g (7oz) finely chopped best quality dark
    chocolate*
finely grated zest of 1 orange
300ml (10 1/2 fl oz) cream
4 tablespoons grappa or brandy

Preheat the oven to 200°C (400°F). Put the rhubarb into a shallow roasting dish and add the sugar and wine. Place in the oven for 25 minutes until the rhubarb is tender. Do not stir so that the rhubarb stays intact in separate pieces. Drain the liquid off the rhubarb and reserve it. Cool the rhubarb.

Line a 23cm (9in) diameter springform tin with plastic food wrap and put half the sponge fingers in a layer on the bottom. Evenly sprinkle half the liquid from the rhubarb over the sponge fingers. Put the pieces of rhubarb in an even layer on top of the biscuits.

Mix the ricotta, half the amaretti, half the chocolate and the orange zest and put this in an even layer on top of the rhubarb. Put the other half of the sponge fingers in a layer on top of the ricotta and sprinkle the remaining half of the rhubarb liquid over the top. Cover and refrigerate for 4 hours or overnight.

When ready to serve the cake, whip the cream with the grappa. Uncover the cake and invert it onto a flat plate or platter. Peel off the plastic food wrap. Spread the cream on top of the cake, then sprinkle with the remaining chocolate and amaretti. Serve in wedges.

or *use ripe peeled sliced peaches or nectarines
    and dessert wine instead of the rhubarb liquid*
or *use mascarpone instead of ricotta for a
    richer cake*
or *if you are in a hurry, assemble the cake in a
    shallow bowl and eat immediately like a trifle.*

Walnut Cake with Dried Figs and Blue Cheese

This is a grown-up dessert of things that are rich but not too sweet. It makes a fabulous end to a meal when presented on a big platter.

The cake is very easy to make. Make sure the walnuts you use are fresh, as rancid walnuts are not nice at all and are often the reason why people say they don't like walnuts. Fresh walnuts are creamy in colour, taste and texture and have a sweet, nutty aroma. *Serves 6*

Cake

180g (6 ¹/₂ oz) butter, melted
180g (6 ¹/₂ oz) brown sugar
3 eggs, beaten
180g (6 ¹/₂ oz) plain flour
1 teaspoon baking powder
150g (5oz) walnut halves
finely grated zest of 1 orange

Preheat the oven to 180°C (350°F). Butter the inside of a 20cm (8in) diameter springform cake tin and line the bottom with baking paper.

Mix the butter, sugar and eggs well. Stir in the remaining ingredients, and pour into the tin. Bake for 45 minutes, or until a skewer pushed into the middle comes out clean. Remove from the oven and cool. Remove from the tin.

Accompaniments

18 dried figs
350g (12 ¹/₂ oz) wedge of your favourite
  blue cheese (I like gorgonzola with this)

Put the cake on a big white platter, put the cheese beside it and pile the figs around it. Give everyone a plate and a knife (and fork if you want to be French about it). Be ceremonious and cut the cake and cheese at the table and let everyone help themselves.

or *serve with a glass of port*
or *use almonds and lemon zest in the cake instead of walnuts and orange, and serve the cake with ripe Beurre Bosc pears and runny brie*
or *serve the cake warm from the oven with mascarpone and fresh dates poached until gooey in a little brown sugar and water.*

Venetian Chocolate Cake with Coffee Granita

I like chocolate cakes to taste like chocolate not cocoa, so naturally they need to be made with chocolate. This cake is one of the best and is based on a recipe from the cooking school at the legendary Hotel Cipriani in Venice.

Coffee Granita is simply sweetened espresso, mixed as it freezes to a highly caffeinated slush. It goes well with the cake and a big dollop of whipped cream. *Serves 6*

Cake
*265g (9 1/2 oz) best-quality dark chocolate,
  chopped*
135g (4 3/4 oz) unsalted butter
4 eggs, separated
210g (7 1/2 oz) castor sugar
1 tablespoon plain flour
1 teaspoon pure vanilla extract
1 teaspoon baking powder

Preheat the oven to 180°C (350°C). Butter and flour a 20cm (8in) springform tin.

Put the chocolate and butter into a heatproof bowl and put the bowl over gently simmering water, stirring the chocolate and butter occasionally until it has melted and is smooth.

Beat the egg yolks and sugar together until pale and fluffy. Stir in the flour, vanilla and baking powder. Stir in the chocolate mixture.

In a separate bowl, whisk the egg whites to soft peaks. Fold the whites into the chocolate mixture and pour into the tin. Bake for 30 minutes. The cake will remain quite soft and moist.

Remove from the oven, cool, then carefully take the cake out of the tin and put it onto a serving plate.

Coffee Granita
125g (4 1/2 oz) sugar
500ml (18fl oz) hot strong espresso coffee
*300ml (10 1/2 fl oz) cream whipped with
  2 tablespoons icing sugar*

Dissolve the sugar in the hot coffee and let it cool. Pour it into a flat tray and put it into the freezer. As it freezes, stir it frequently so that it does not freeze into a block, but into a slushy mass of large ice crystals. If it does freeze too much, break it up, quickly place it into a food processor and process until it looks like snow, then return to the freezer for 15 minutes before serving.

Cut the cake into wedges. Put a spoonful of whipped cream in the bottom of each of six small cold glasses or bowls. Pile some granita on top and top with a spoonful of whipped cream. Serve immediately with a wedge of cake.

or *serve the cake with Oranges in Red Wine Syrup (see page 140)*
or *serve the granita by itself after a spicy meal*
or *omit the granita and carefully slice the cake into two halves horizontally, fill it like a sponge cake with whipped cream and fresh raspberries and serve dusted with icing sugar.*

Orange and Almond Cake with Almond Cream and Salade d'Oranges

This is inspired by an Elizabeth David recipe. It is a beautiful, fragrant orange cake similar to those found in Sephardic Jewish cuisine. Whenever I make it I am astonished at how good it is and can never decide whether it is a delicious French pastry or an Arabic confection. *Serves 6–8*

Cake

60g (2oz) dry breadcrumbs, plus extra
  for dusting
125g (4 ½ oz) castor sugar
3 eggs, separated
pinch of flaky sea salt
1 tablespoon orange flower water
juice of 3 oranges
finely grated zest of 2 oranges
125g (4 ½ oz) ground almonds
icing sugar and ground cinnamon
  for dusting

Preheat the oven to 180°C (350°F). Butter and dust with breadcrumbs a 20cm (8in) diameter spring-form cake tin.

Beat the sugar, egg yolks and salt together until white. Mix in the orange flower water, juice, orange zest, almonds and breadcrumbs.

Beat the egg whites until stiff and fold them into the other mixture. Pour into the tin and bake for 40 minutes or until a skewer comes out clean. Remove from the oven and cool. Dust with icing sugar and a little cinnamon.

Almond Cream

3 tablespoons cornflour
900ml (1 ½ pt) full-cream milk
3 tablespoons orange flower water
150g (5oz) castor sugar
1 teaspoon pure vanilla extract
4 tablespoons ground blanched almonds
finely grated zest of 1 orange

Mix the cornflour with 100ml (3½ fl oz) of the milk.

Put the remaining milk, orange flower water, sugar, vanilla, almonds and orange zest into a saucepan and bring to the boil. Add the cornflour, stirring continuously. Simmer for 2–3 minutes or until thickened. Strain into a bowl, cool and chill.

Whisk until smooth before serving.

Oranges

6 oranges, peeled and thinly sliced
  into rounds
6 fresh dates, stoned and thinly sliced
6 tablespoons icing sugar
1 teaspoon ground cinnamon
finely grated zest of 1 orange
mint leaves
rose petals or jasmine flowers

Spread the orange slices and dates onto a serving platter. Sprinkle with icing sugar, cinnamon and orange zest. Chill well. Serve garnished with mint leaves, rose petals or jasmine.

Serve the cake in wedges with the orange salad on the side and the Almond Cream poured over the cake.

or *add sliced peaches, berries, fresh cherries, pomegranate seeds or sliced apricots to the salad*
or *use the Almond Cream as the custard in a trifle with strawberries as the fruit.*

Passionfruit Jelly with Passionfruit Syrup and Bananas

I love jellies and this one is exquisite, as the tanginess of the jelly goes well with the creaminess of the bananas. It is perfect in a refreshing, mouth-cleansing way after a spicy meal.

Make the Passionfruit Syrup if fresh passionfruit are available, otherwise use bought passionfruit in syrup straight from the jar. *Serves 6*

Jelly
500ml (18fl oz) dry Riesling
1 piece lemon peel, no pith
100g (3 1/2 oz) castor sugar
200ml (7fl oz) passionfruit in syrup, pips
strained out and discarded, or the pulp
from 4 passionfruit, pushed through a
sieve and pips discarded
1 tablespoon powdered gelatine

Bring the Riesling, peel, sugar and passionfruit syrup or pulp to the boil over a moderate heat, stirring until the sugar is dissolved. When boiling, whisk in the gelatine, stirring until completely dissolved.

Remove from the heat, discard the peel, and pour into six 100ml-capacity moulds. Refrigerate until set – about 4 hours.

Syrup
200g (7oz) sugar
4 tablespoons water
juice of 1 orange
pulp from 5 passionfruit
4 bananas, peeled and sliced for garnish

Put the sugar, water and orange juice into a small saucepan and bring to the boil. Stir well to dissolve the sugar, remove from the heat and stir in the passionfruit. Cool and chill.

To serve, unmould each jelly onto a small plate and serve with sliced bananas and the passionfruit syrup spooned over.

or *serve with mangoes and coconut cream*
instead of bananas
or *serve with strawberries and whipped cream*
instead of bananas
or *serve as a centrepiece by making one large*
jelly and presenting it on a large platter
surrounded by sliced bananas and other fruit.

Strawberry, Lemon and Grappa Trifle

This boozy trifle is really like a tiramisu construction, or rather deconstruction, using different flavourings. In this case strawberries, lemon and grappa are layered with sponge fingers and topped with a mix of mascarpone, cream and eggs. If you can't get grappa, use brandy. This has a fair amount of alcohol in it so you should probably keep it away from the children. *Serves 6*

500g (1lb 2oz) strawberries, hulled and halved
200g (7oz) castor sugar
juice and zest of 1 large lemon
250g (8 ³/₄ oz) packet sponge fingers or savoiardi biscuits
4 tablespoons grappa, plus plenty for sprinkling
2 eggs, separated
250g (8 ³/₄ oz) mascarpone
300ml (10 ¹/₂ fl oz) cream
chopped best-quality dark chocolate for garnish

Put the strawberries, half the sugar, the lemon zest and juice into a bowl and mix well. Set aside, mixing occasionally to dissolve the sugar.

Put a layer of sponge fingers in the bottom of a wide bowl and sprinkle them with plenty of grappa. Spread the strawberry mixture evenly over the sponge fingers.

Put the egg yolks, the remaining sugar and 4 tablespoons of grappa into a bowl and beat until pale and fluffy.

In another bowl beat the mascarpone and cream until whipped.

In another bowl beat the egg whites until stiff.

Fold the egg yolk mix, mascarpone mix and egg whites together. Spread this mixture over the top of the strawberries. Sprinkle chopped chocolate over everything. Place in the refrigerator and chill completely for at least 1 hour. The biscuits need to soften a little.

or use any sort of fresh or thawed frozen berries in this dish
or use sliced fresh peaches and orange juice instead of lemon juice
or use small dishes or glasses and make individual trifles for a special dinner – top each with a perfect strawberry with the green hull still attached.

Frutas de Hacienda Guzman

The following are three fruit salads I once ate in southern Spain. They were served in separate bowls but all at the same time. They are so simple they are hardly even recipes, but they are perfect after a large meal when the weather is hot. *Serves 6*

Oranges in Red Wine Syrup

250ml (9fl oz) red wine
100g (3 1/2 oz) sugar
6 cloves
1 cinnamon stick
5 oranges, peeled and thinly sliced
1/2 a crystallised orange, thinly sliced
  (optional)

Bring the wine, sugar, cloves and cinnamon to the boil. Remove the syrup from the heat and let it cool completely.

Put the orange slices and the crystallised orange, if using, into a bowl. Pour the syrup over everything and chill.

Watermelon

1/2 a small watermelon (enough for
  6 small portions), peeled and cut into
  small bite-sized chunks, discarding
  the pips
muscovado sugar for sprinkling

Put the watermelon into a bowl and sprinkle well with the sugar.

Honeydew Melon

1 ripe Honeydew or other green melon,
  peeled, seeded and cut into small
  bite-sized chunks
Pernod or Ricard (aniseed flavoured spirit)
icing sugar for sprinkling

Put the melon into a bowl and sprinkle well with Pernod or Ricard and plenty of icing sugar.

or serve the fruit salads with good-quality vanilla ice cream, whipped cream or Greek yoghurt

or serve the watermelon with a liberal sprinkling of sweet sherry or port

or add a handful of raisins to the wine syrup for the oranges.

Sherry and Almond Ice with Extremadura Fruit Compote

Extremadura is the mountainous south-western area of Spain renowned for good food. On a trip there I stayed at the paradore in Jarandilla de la Vera. Paradores are government-run hotels which were set up often in old castles and the like to preserve them, to give work to the locals and to use the local produce. One night in Jarandilla de la Vera they served a creamy scoop of ice cream on a compote of jewel-like berries – it was one of the best things I'd tasted. Here is my approximation.

The 'ice' is not ice cream but more like a semifreddo, which means it can be made without an ice cream machine. As it contains fresh eggs, it is not meant to be kept. You make it and eat it.

While the berries in the original compote were wild berries gathered in the countryside around the paradore, bought fresh or frozen berries work just fine. *Serves 6–8*

Sherry and Almond Ice

3 eggs
100g (3 1/2 oz) sugar
1 teaspoon pure vanilla extract
200g (7oz) mascarpone
300ml (10 1/2 fl oz) cream
50ml (2fl oz) sweet dark sherry, plus extra
    for drizzling
150g (5oz) roughly chopped roasted
    almonds

Beat the eggs, sugar and vanilla until they are pale and thick.

In a separate bowl, beat the mascarpone, cream and sherry until whipped.

Fold together the yolk mixture, the almonds and the cream mixture. Freeze for about 4 hours until frozen.

Serve scoops sprinkled with extra sherry and the following fruit compote.

Fruit Compote

1 orange, sliced
1 apple and 1 pear peeled, cored and
    thinly sliced
300g (10 1/2 oz) sugar
1 stick cinnamon
zest of 1 lemon
250ml (9fl oz) red wine
250g (8 3/4 oz) blueberries
250g (8 3/4 oz) raspberries

Put the unpeeled orange slices in a saucepan, cover with boiling water and simmer for 5 minutes, then drain well.

Bring all the ingredients, except the berries, to the boil and simmer until the apples and pears are tender. Add the berries, bring back to the boil, and remove from the heat. Cool and chill.

Serve the Sherry and Almond Ice on top of the Fruit Compote.

or   use the compote as the fruit part of a trifle
or   serve the fruit with toasted brioche and Greek
    yoghurt for a special brunch
or   add a handful of finely chopped dark
    chocolate to the ice.

Almond Brioche with Lemon Granita and Whipped Cream

In Sicily a traditional way of eating granita is to stuff it into a split brioche, often for breakfast. Brioche is easy to make – it is just a cake risen with yeast. There is no tedious kneading and you can beat it mercilessly to get the batter smooth with no ill effects. The most important thing to remember is that the milk needs to be lukewarm or at blood heat (as warm as you are). If it is too hot, it will kill the yeast, and if it is too cold, the yeast will not start to work. *Serves 6*

Brioche
150ml (5fl oz) lukewarm milk
1 teaspoon dried yeast
4 organic eggs, beaten
250g (8 3/4 oz) plain flour
50g (2oz) finely ground blanched almonds
50g (2oz) thinly sliced almonds
finely grated zest of 1 lemon
pinch of flaky sea salt
3 tablespoons sugar
150g (5oz) unsalted butter, softened but
   not melted
icing sugar for dusting

Lemon Granita
200g (7oz) sugar
600ml (1pt) water
finely grated zest of 1 lemon
juice of 3 lemons

Put the milk and yeast into a warm mixing bowl. Do not stir it, but wait about 5 minutes until the yeast softens and then stir to dissolve.

Beat in the eggs, flour, the ground and sliced almonds, lemon zest, salt and sugar until you have a smooth batter. Cover and put in a warm, draught-free place to rise until doubled in bulk.

Preheat the oven to 180°C (350°F). Butter and flour a 12 x 50ml (2fl oz) volume muffin tray or 12 small individual moulds.

Beat the butter until smooth. When the dough has risen, beat in the butter until well incorporated, with no lumps remaining. Pour into the tins and put in a warm place until you see the dough begin to rise again.

Place in the oven and bake for 15–20 minutes or until a skewer pushed in the middle of a brioche comes out clean. Remove from the tins and dust well with icing sugar.

Put the sugar, water and lemon zest into a saucepan and bring to the boil. Simmer for 10 minutes, remove from the heat and cool.

Add the juice and pour into a shallow metal tray. As it freezes, stir it frequently so that it does not freeze into a block, but into a slushy mass of large ice crystals. If it does freeze too much, break it up, quickly place it into a food processor and process until it looks like snow, then return to the freezer for 15 minutes before serving.

Serve the brioche split with some granita in it or with a small bowl or glass of granita with whipped cream on the side.

or *make the brioche in a loaf tin, then serve toasted sliced with fresh berries, a liberal dusting of icing sugar and mascarpone*
or *granita can be made from fruit juices such as orange, mango, grape, pineapple, apple or apricot – just sweeten if necessary and freeze, stirring to stop it forming into a block*
or *turn the brioche into a savarin by making it in a ring mould. Make the granita but double the amount of sugar so that you have a lemon syrup. Pour the syrup over the cooked savarin, cool and chill. Pile peeled, sliced fresh peaches or nectarines into the centre of the savarin and serve with whipped cream.*

Barbecued Sticky Rice Pudding

Barbecued rice pudding sounds like an impossibility, but what this really means is that you can cook it on the barbecue. (You could also cook it in the oven if you want to.) It is one of those dishes that, once put together, will cook itself and can go on the barbecue after you have cooked dinner on it, cleaned it and retired to the table to eat. By the time you have finished your main course a hot rice pudding will be waiting for you. *Serves 6*

250g (8 3/4 oz) glutinous white rice
50g (2oz) long grain white rice
pinch of flaky sea salt
4 tablespoons finely grated palm sugar
350ml (12 1/2 fl oz) water
6 x 25cm square pieces each of baking
    paper and tin foil for wrapping
butter
finely grated zest of 1 lemon
6 tablespoons blackcurrant jam
200g (7oz) blueberries
400ml (14fl oz) thick canned
    coconut cream

Wash the rices well and soak them together for 30 minutes. Put the rices, salt, palm sugar and water into a small saucepan and bring to the boil, turn the heat to the lowest setting, cover tightly, and cook, without uncovering for any reason, for 20 minutes. Remove from the heat and let it stand, without uncovering, for 5 minutes. Uncover and gently fluff up, being careful not to mash the rice.

Butter one side of each of the squares of paper. For each pudding, put a square of paper, butter side up, on top of a square of foil. Put one-sixth of the rice on the paper, sprinkle with a little lemon zest, 1 tablespoon of the jam, one-sixth of the blueberries and 2 tablespoons of coconut cream. Wrap into a parcel like a spring roll by folding in the sides and rolling up.

Cook the parcels on a moderate barbecue for 15–20 minutes until very hot.

Open the parcels and serve with the remaining coconut cream.

or *instead of jam and blueberries, use extra palm sugar and slices of fresh mango*
or *if cooking the pudding in the oven, simply put all the ingredients together in an ovenproof casserole, cover, and bake until hot*
or *use crystallised ginger and long strand desiccated coconut instead of jam and blueberries.*

Banana and Chocolate Bread and Butter Pudding

Bread and butter puddings using sliced white supermarket bread will always taste flabby and insipid. Use good bread and you will be astounded at what a delectably rich pudding it makes. This pudding is merely buttered slices of bread with a filling set in a baked custard. You can make one large pudding or individual ones. Once you have mastered the method for making this kind of bread and butter pudding, the combination of flavours can be endless. *Serves 6*

4 eggs

*125g (4 1/2 oz) raw sugar, plus extra
    for sprinkling*

1 teaspoon pure vanilla extract

750ml (1 pt 5fl oz) milk

*3/4 loaf good French bread, sliced
    2cm (1in) thick*

150g (5oz) butter, melted

3 bananas, sliced

150g (5oz) dark chocolate, chopped

Preheat the oven to 190°C (375°F). Beat the eggs, sugar, vanilla and milk together. Reserve.

Brush the bread slices with plenty of melted butter. Put half of them, butter side down, into an ovenproof dish. I use one 20cm (8in) in diameter and about 9cm (3 1/2 in) deep.

Spread the bananas and chocolate over the top, reserving some of the chocolate. Put the remaining bread slices on top, butter side up.

Pour the egg mixture on top of the bread. Push the bread down under the egg mixture and let it spring back to soak it up. Sprinkle the top with the reserved chocolate and plenty of extra sugar. Set aside for 10 minutes to soak.

Place in the oven and bake for 45 minutes until well set, puffed and golden. Serve hot with whipped cream.

or *for a richer pudding use sliced croissants or
    brioche instead of bread*

or *use sliced pears and stoned fresh dates
    instead of the bananas and chocolate*

or *when the pudding is cooked and out of the
    oven, sprinkle it liberally with whisky, brandy
    or rum for a truly grown-up version.*

Gula Melaka

Whatever you may think of how Singapore has changed, it still has one of the most unique and dynamic food cultures in the world. I go to Singapore to eat the wonderful food, a pastime I feel is deeply satisfying. Indian, Malay, Indonesian, Nonya and many varieties of Chinese food are all specialities of Singapore.

Accomplished Singaporean foodwriter and cook Connie Clarkson once gave me the invaluable gift of spending a week showing me the food of Singapore. It totally changed my understanding of Asian food. One of the typical dishes we sampled was Gula Melaka. Three very simple components – the velvety textured sago, the caramelly sweet palm sugar syrup and the rich coconut cream – combine to create a cooling, refreshing dessert that is perfect after a rich or spicy meal.

Gula Melaka is at the same time the name of the dish and the name of the palm sugar used. *Serves 6*

Sago

100g (3 ½ oz) sago, rinsed in cold water
350ml (12 ½ fl oz) water
pinch of flaky sea salt

Bring the water to the boil, add the salt and sago and stir continuously. Reduce the heat and simmer until the sago is transparent and the mixture is thick – about 5 minutes. Pour into about six 75ml (3fl oz) moulds and cool completely. Cover well and refrigerate until set (overnight is fine).

Palm Sugar Syrup

300g (10 ½ oz) dark palm sugar
  (gula melaka), grated
250ml (9fl oz) water

Bring the sugar and water to the boil in a small saucepan, and simmer until all the sugar has dissolved. Remove from the heat, cool and chill.

Accompaniment

400ml (14fl oz) thick canned coconut
  cream

Serve the sago well chilled, unmoulded in a small glass or dish. Pour plenty of Palm Sugar Syrup over each and serve the coconut cream separately for pouring.

or you could serve some tropical fruit with this dish – pineapple, mangoes, lychees, guavas, feijoas or pomegranates would be suitable – but this dessert is so perfect and traditional that I am reluctant to tamper with it.

Olive Oil Chocolate Mousse

This recipe is my version of a dessert made by Gabriela Llamas, the accomplished chef who runs the Alambique cooking school in Madrid. A chocolate mousse with olive oil and no cream sounds far-fetched, but it works perfectly. It shows the Spanish love of chocolate (the original recipe was double this amount and she said it served six!) and the innovative use of Spain's other great product, olive oil. Unlike mousses made with cream, this one has a chewy, nougaty texture.

Do not choose an oil with a peppery or strong grassy flavour – I use a sweet and nutty Spanish extra virgin olive oil from the supermarket for this recipe.

The Chocolate Shards method is an easy technique for making thin, jagged pieces of chocolate which are great for decorating all sorts of sweet dishes. *Serves 6*

Mousse

150g (5 oz) good-quality dark chocolate
125ml (4fl oz) extra virgin olive oil
4 eggs, separated
125g (4 1/2 oz) castor sugar
1 tablespoon Grand Marnier or other
   orange liqueur
pinch of flaky sea salt

Melt the chocolate in a bowl over very hot, but not boiling water, then slowly stir in the olive oil until well combined. Set aside.

Beat the egg yolks with half the sugar until pale and fluffy. Mix the chocolate mixture with the egg yolk mixture and stir in the Grand Marnier.

Whip the egg whites and salt until stiff and continue whipping, adding the remaining sugar gradually until it is all incorporated.

Fold the egg white mixture into the chocolate mixture. Pour into a large bowl or individual cups or dishes and chill for at least 4 hours.

Chocolate Shards

baking paper
200g (7 oz) good quality dark chocolate,
   finely chopped

Preheat the oven to 200°C (400°F).

Take a large sheet of baking paper that will fit onto the baking tray. Put one-quarter of the chopped chocolate in the middle and cover with another sheet of baking paper the same size. Put into the oven until the chocolate just melts.

Remove from the oven and carefully roll over the top sheet of paper with a rolling pin so that the melted chocolate is flattened into a thin, but not too thin, sheet. Carefully lift the paper, still sandwiched together with the chocolate, into the fridge to harden. Keep it flat.

Repeat with the remaining chocolate and more baking paper.

When hard, peel off the paper and break the chocolate into large jagged pieces.

Just before serving the mousse, decorate with Chocolate Shards.

or use the mousse as a filling for a chocolate cake
or serve it with fresh raspberries.

Spanish Chocolate with Almendrados

The Spanish have an amazing sweet tooth – they actually serve chocolate like this for breakfast! It is a chocolate-lover's delight and staggeringly rich, but very easy to make.

Almendrados, almond meringue cakes, seem to be in every bakery in Spain, and reflect the Arab influence on food there. *Serves 6*

Spanish Chocolate
375ml (13fl oz) cream
1/2 teaspoon ground cinnamon
300g (10 1/2 oz) finely chopped
  good-quality dark chocolate
2 tablespoons brandy
whipped cream for garnish

Put the cream and cinnamon into a small saucepan and bring to the boil. Add the chocolate and brandy and stir until dissolved. The mixture should be thick and creamy.

Pour into six small cups and top each with a spoonful of whipped cream.

Almendrados
3 large egg whites
300g (10 1/2 oz) castor sugar
finely grated zest of 1 lemon
1/2 teaspoon ground cloves
250g (8 3/4 oz) toasted slivered almonds
50g icing sugar mixed with 1 tablespoon
  of ground cinnamon for dusting

Preheat the oven to 110°C (225°F).

Beat the egg whites until stiff and slowly add the sugar little by little until it is all incorporated. Mix in the lemon zest and cloves. The mixture should be very thick. Fold in the almonds.

Fill 20 small paper cases with the mixture and bake for 1 hour until cracked and crisp. Remove from the oven and dust well with the icing sugar/cinnamon mix. If storing, store in an airtight tin and dust when needed.
Makes about 20

Serve cups of Spanish Chocolate with the Almendrados on the side.

or *even though it may sound depraved adding to something so rich, the warm chocolate can be used as a sauce on vanilla bean ice cream*

or *serve the Almendrados with short black coffee instead of the chocolate for a lighter finish to a meal*

or *instead of making the Almendrados in paper cases, divide the mix in half and shape each half into a 20cm (8in) diameter disc-shape on two buttered and floured baking trays. Bake until cracked and crisp, cool, then fill like a sandwich with strawberries or raspberries and whipped cream. Leave to soften for an hour in the refrigerator and serve cut into wedges.*

Ricotta Sandwich with Peaches in White Wine

Another type of sweet sandwich, this time a simple homemade sponge cake put together with a mixture of ricotta and crumbled almond amaretti biscuits (available from supermarkets and specialty food shops) and served with marinated peaches and whipped cream or Greek yoghurt. Prepare the peaches a day in advance. *Serves 6*

Peaches

*6 large ripe peaches (white if possible),
    peeled, stoned and sliced*
250ml (9fl oz) fruity white wine
200g (7oz) castor sugar

Mix everything together in a non-reactive bowl, cover and refrigerate overnight.

Sponge

oil for the cake tin
4 eggs
100g (3 1/2 oz) castor sugar
finely grated zest of 1 orange
100g (3 1/2 oz) plain flour

Preheat the oven to 180°C (350°F). Lightly oil and paper two 20cm (8in) diameter cake tins.

Beat the eggs, sugar and orange zest until pale and doubled in bulk. Fold in the flour and pour half the mixture into each tin. Bake for 10–15 minutes until a skewer comes out clean. Cool and remove the paper.

Ricotta Filling

400g (14oz) ricotta, beaten smooth
10 amaretti biscuits, crumbled

Mix the ricotta and amaretti together.

Spread the ricotta filling over one cake, top with the other cake and put it onto a large platter. Pile the peaches and syrup on top. Dust with icing sugar. Serve with whipped cream.

or *use a mixture of fruit instead of peaches – nectarines, strawberries, ripe pears, cherries, apricots and blueberries are all suitable*
or *the peaches are great as a topping for vanilla ice cream or simply with mascarpone*
or *turn the sponge into a simple cream sponge by sandwiching with sliced strawberries and cream and dusting the top with icing sugar. It is also perfect for a trifle and, instead of the orange peel, it can be flavoured with such things as vanilla, cocoa, lemon zest, ground almonds or spice.*

glossary

Al dente refers to pasta cooked in plenty of boiling salted water until tender (but not overcooked) to the bite.

Amchoor is a deliciously sour powder made from finely ground green mangoes – available from Indian food shops.

Baking blind means baking an empty uncooked pastry case before you fill it with a sweet or savoury filling. Place a sheet of tin foil, shiny side down, on the base of the pastry and cover with dried beans, rice or gravel (or anything clean that won't burn). Bake in a preheated oven (180°C) for 20 minutes until the edges of the pastry turn golden brown. Remove from the oven and lift out the baking blind material, including the tin foil. Put the pastry shell back in the oven for a further 10 minutes to make sure the bottom is cooked.

Broad beans are nicer peeled – use them fresh or frozen.

Carbonossi, also known as kabanos, are mild garlic sausages – usually found in the deli section of the supermarket.

Chickpea flour, also known as besan, is made from finely ground chickpeas – available from Indian food shops.

Chinese five spice powder is a fragrant mixture, usually made up of cinnamon, cloves, Szechuan peppercorns, fennel seeds and star anise – available from Asian food shops.

Chinese salted black beans are also known as fermented black beans – available from Asian food shops.

Fish sauce is used in South-East Asian cookery for an interesting and complex salty flavour – available from Asian food shops.

Ginger juice is easily made by finely grating fresh ginger, then squeezing the juice out with your hands.

Gula melaka, also known as palm sugar, is widely used in Asian cooking. It is made from palm tree sap and can range in colour from creamy white to dark brown. Its consistency varies from soft and sticky to hard and dense – available from Asian food shops.

Japanese green tea soba noodles (often used in soup) are made from buckwheat, plain flour and green tea powder – available from Asian food shops.

Jointing a chicken is best done with a Chinese cleaver – start by cutting down each side of the backbone (discard the backbone or reserve it for stock), then cut off the legs and wings from each half. Cut these in half again, discarding the wing tips (also good for adding to the stockpot), then cut each half of the breast in two – you should end up with 12 pieces of chicken.

Kaffir lime leaves offer an intense lime aroma that is excellent in many dishes, Asian or otherwise – available fresh, frozen and dried from specialist food shops and some supermarkets.

Kecap manis is a sweet, sticky Indonesian soy sauce – available from Asian food shops.

Marsala, a Sicilian specialty, is a fortified wine obtainable either sweet or dry – available from wine shops.

Mirin, with its low alcohol content, is a sweet Japanese rice wine used in cooking – available from Asian food shops.

Miso, a fermented paste of soy beans, salt and rice (or barley), comes in varying strengths; the lighter it is in colour (e.g. shiro-miso), the milder the flavour – available from Asian food shops.

Noodles come in various shapes and sizes and can be made from different starches including wheat, rice flour and mung beans. Cellophane noodles, also known as cellophane and Lungkow noodles, are made from the latter – all are available from Asian food shops.

Nori is an edible seaweed that comes in paper thin sheets used mostly for making sushi – available from Asian food shops.

Orange flower water, also known as orange blossom water, is made from the distilled flowers of orange trees. It has a concentrated perfume and flavour (so use sparingly) and appears in many Mediterranean and Middle Eastern sweet dishes, including cakes, puddings and fruit salads – available from specialist food shops.

Palm sugar – see gula melaka

Pancetta, meaning 'little stomach' in Italian, is a type of salt-cured belly pork closely related to bacon – available in specialist food shops and many supermarkets.

Paprika, the Spanish smoked variety, is deep red in colour with an intoxicating smoky aroma. It comes in three different delicious flavours: sweet, bittersweet and hot – all of which are available in specialist food shops and many supermarkets.

Parmesan cheese is available in different grades from specialist food shops as well as supermarkets. For good results buy the best quality you can afford. The best Italian grade, parmigiano reggiano, is name controlled.

Polenta, or cornmeal porridge, is the quintessential northern Italian comfort food. In Italy it's often served as a first course or as a side dish.

Preserved lemons are a quintessential Moroccan ingredient that give a delicious flavour to salads, fish dishes or lamb or chicken stews. They are available from specialist food shops – or you can prepare them yourself as follows. Wash the lemons well, then cut into quarters but not right through the skin or rind so that each lemon holds together. Pack the insides of each cut lemon with lots of coarse sea salt before placing in a clean jar with extra salt. Pour boiling water over the top to cover completely, seal the jar and leave for 1 month before using.

Prosciutto is lightly salted, air-dried Italian-style ham – the real thing (imported from Italy) is available from specialist food shops and is worth the extra money.

Provolone cheese is an Italian mild-tasting cow's milk cheese.

Rice varieties used in this book include plump short grain Calasparra rice (grown in south-eastern Spain), which can absorb up to three times its own volume in liquid and still stay firm, making it ideal for paella and similar dishes, and Italian rice. For risotto, always use Italian rice (also short grained but famous for its creamy starch content – choose from arborio, vialone nano and carnaroli). All these rices are available from specialist food shops and some supermarkets.

Saffron, used internationally in both sweet and savoury dishes, is made from the dried orangy-dark red coloured stigmas of the crocus flower (harvested by hand making it an expensive spice, but well worth the cost as the musky scent and earthy taste will transform many dishes). To get the most out of saffron, gently toast it in a dry pan over a moderate heat until fragrant and just beginning to darken, then remove from pan and cool. Crush to a powder with your fingertips or the back of a spoon before using as directed. Available from specialist food shops and some supermarkets.

Szechuan peppercorns are small red-brown berries that grow on a shrub native to the Szechuan province of China. They are best toasted in a dry pan until fragrant and darkened in colour, then ground as required – available from Asian food shops.

Shao Xing Chinese cooking wine is a common ingredient in Chinese cuisine – available from Asian food shops.

Shrimp paste is made from salted and fermented dried shrimps, a pungent mix used in Asian cooking. It is also known as blachan and kapi (Malaysian and Thai terms respectively) – available from Asian food shops.

Sumac, a dark purplish powder used in Middle Eastern cuisine, is made from the ground berries of the sumac bush and has a spicy, sour flavour – available from Asian or Middle Eastern food shops.

Tamarind pulp has an appetising sour/spicy taste and is used to flavour curries, stews and condiments. It is made from compressed tamarind pods (from the tropical tamarind tree) that have been covered with boiling water and left to steep for 30 minutes, then mixed well and pushed through a sieve – the seeds should be discarded and the resulting pulp allowed to cool before using. Tamarind pulp should not be confused with tamarind concentrate, which has a different consistency and can be bought as a ready-to-use preparation – both the pods and the concentrate are available from Asian food shops.

Vietnamese mint, also known as laksa leaves, is a pungent herb used in many South-East Asian dishes (it should not be confused with common or garden mint) – available fresh and dried from Asian food shops (and can be easily grown from a leaf or cutting).

index

acknowledgements

Once again, thanks to The Studio of Tableware, Auckland, for their help with props. And special thanks to Lois Daish for her valuable input.